How to FLY

THE CONSUMER FEDERATION OF AMERICA'S AIRLINE SURVIVAL GUIDE

By STEPHEN BROBECK
with Jack Gillis

For additional copies of
How to FLY

Sales of How to FLY benefit the Consumer Federation of America, a consumer advocacy organization of over 230 state, local and national consumer interest organizations. Additional copies of the book may be obtained by mail from the Consumer Federation of America. Send a check for $7.95 ($6.95 plus $1 postage and handling) for each copy to:

Consumer Federation of America
1424 16th Street, N.W.
Washington, D.C. 20036

Please make check payable to the Consumer Federation of American and allow 3-4 weeks for delivery.

Note

CONTENTS

ACKNOWLEDGEMENTS

While the guide contains much original research, it also incorporates the excellent work of others. The U.S. Department of Transportation's Office of Community and Consumer Affairs supplied important information on airline practices, consumer complaints, and passenger rights. So did the Aviation Consumer Action Project (ACAP). Three regular publications proved to be especially valuable. "Practical Traveler" columns in *The New York Times*, particularly those by Paul Grimes, contained a wealth of helpful information. Periodically, *USA Today* has published useful carrier ratings and travel recommendations. *Consumer Reports Travel Letter* often has carried information both on general topics and on specific features such as fares or even seat widths.

I could not have completed this guide without the assistance of others. Susan Brobeck and Lisa Goldstein deserve special recognition for their invaluable research and analysis. John Simbeck, Kathleen Governale, Edith Furst, Karen Hoehn, Karen Fierst, Cristina Mendoza, and Alan Fox also made important contributions in these areas. After a draft had been completed, Norm Strickman, Timothy Kelly, John R. Brobeck, Susan Tanzman Kaplan, Carolyn Friede, and Barbara Roper suggested numerous substantive and stylistic improvements. These changes were made to the manuscript by Tanny Southerland. Additional typing support was provided by Teresa Wooten-Talley and Bill North-Rudin. The credit for design and graphic preparation goes to Susan Cole. Special thanks go to Karen Steinke for her assistance in typesetting, and to Stacey Hosler of BookCrafters for her patience and flexibility. But my greatest debt is to Jack Gillis, who assisted on all phases of preparing this guide.

Stephen Brobeck
November, 1987

INTRODUCTION

For many airline passengers, the "friendly skies" have become anything but friendly. Passengers find it difficult to obtain information on flights and fares. At the airport, they often wait in long lines at ticket counters. At the gate, they may learn that their flight has been delayed or cancelled. Or they may discover that, because of over-booking, they won't get a seat.

On the airplane, harried flight attendants may provide perfunctory service. In the air, passengers are exposed to health threats ranging from cigarette smoke to viruses. Throughout the flight, they may worry about the possibility of a crash. Then their relief after a safe landing may turn to anger when their luggage doesn't appear.

Yet, the "brave new world" of deregulated airlines presents opportunities as well as risks. Extraordinarily low fares are still available to many who plan in advance. On popular routes, there are often several carriers from which to choose. Moreover, frequent flyer programs offer the possibility of first-class upgrades and free airline tickets.

In brief, airline travel is more complicated than it has ever been. If travelers are going to fly conveniently, comfortably, and inexpensively, they must learn about the new realities of flying – the problems as well as the opportunities.

This book was written to assist this effort. It covers every aspect of flying on domestic routes – from dealing with a travel agent to coping with delays to traveling with young children. Its chapters and airline and airport profiles contain the most up-to-date information, as of early fall 1987, on these and other subjects. It also provides useful information on all major carriers, including performance ratings.

1

RATING THE AIRLINES

Which Airlines Offer the Best Service and Lowest Fares

Traditionally, consumers have come to expect a trade-off between service and cost. For air travel, you don't necessarily have to make that tradeoff. In fact, business travelers often complain that they are paying twice as much as the passenger they are sitting next to, for exactly the same service.

This chapter will help you understand the difference in service and prices, evaluate how the airlines stack up in each area, and give you the information you need to make the best choice considering both factors.

RATING CUSTOMER SERVICE

The best measure of customer service is the number of complaints received by the U.S. Department of Transportation about individual airlines. These grievances run the gamut, from flight delays and cancellations to lost luggage to rude treatment by airline employees.

To use these complaints as an index of customer dissatisfaction, we adjusted them for the number of passengers carried by each airline. The following table lists each airline's complaint index number, the ratio of complaints made to DOT in 1986 and the first half of 1987 per 100,000 passengers. The higher the number, the poorer the service.

The table also contains a customer service rating. We gave *good* evaluations to airlines with a ratio under 1.00, *fair* to those with ratios between 1.00 and 1.99, *poor* to those with ratios between 2.00 and 3.99, and *very poor* to those with ratings over 4.00. Only three airlines earned good ratings – Alaska, Delta, and Southwest. Five airlines had very poor evaluations – Continental, Eastern, Northwest, Pan American, and TWA. Although these ratings may seem harsh, by all accounts customer service during this rating period was not good.

SERVICE RATINGS

Airline	Complaints per 100,000 Passengers	Rating
Alaska	0.85	Good
America West	1.38	Fair
American	1.88	Fair
Braniff	2.71	Poor
Continental	13.47	Very Poor
Delta	0.93	Good
Eastern	4.65	Very Poor
Hawaiian	3.70	Poor
Midway	2.12	Poor
Northwest	5.83	Very Poor
PSA	1.13	Fair
Pan American	5.74	Very Poor
Piedmont	1.41	Fair
Southwest	0.62	Good
TWA	5.71	Very Poor
United	3.47	Poor
USAir	1.70	Fair

RATING THE FARES

Rating fare levels offered by individual airlines is much more difficult than evaluating service. This is because all airlines do not fly the same routes, and on each route they typically offer a variety of fares subject to a number of constraints.

In order to help consumers determine which airlines, on the average, offer the best fares, we developed an overall fare rating based on a comparison of fares charged by 18 major airlines on 17 popular routes. We assigned each airline a fare rating index based on a comparison of each company's average fares. (See the note below for details on how the ratings were developed.)

The higher the index, the higher you can expect the average fares to be on that airline. One dollar sign was assigned for each 10 percentage points – the fewer dollar signs, the lower the fares.

A Note on the Rating System: The ratings are based on a comparison of 17 popular routes, including: Chicago-Denver, Chicago-Dallas/Ft. Worth, Chicago-Los Angeles, Dallas/Ft. Worth-Los Angeles, Houston-San Antonio, Los Angeles-Honolulu, Los Angeles-San Francisco, New York-Chicago, New York-Miami, Phoenix-Los Angeles, Seattle-Anchorage, San Francisco-Anchorage, San Francisco-Honolulu, San Francisco-Seattle, St. Louis-Los Angeles, Washington-Boston, and Washington-Chicago. We included 448 coach and discount coach fares (except night coach) purchased two days in advance.

All the fares offered by each airline were averaged for each route. Then the lowest average fare was given an index of zero, and the average fare of each of the airlines was assigned an index representing a percentage it was above this lowest fare. Finally, for each airline the percentages on all routes were averaged. The lower this average percentage, the lower the typical fares.

Percentages between 0 and 9 were given a one dollar sign rating; those between 10 and 19, two dollar signs; those between 20 and 29, three dollar signs; those between

30 and 39, four dollar signs; and those over 40, five dollar signs. The smaller the number of dollar signs, the lower the fares.

FARE RATINGS

Airline	Number of Routes	Percentage Index	Fare Rating
Alaska	4	24%	$$$
America West	4	18%	$$
American	13	48%	$$$$$
Braniff	3	3%	$
Continental	9	27%	$$$
Delta	9	37%	$$$$
Eastern	4	13%	$$
Hawaiian	2	31%	$$$$
Midway	4	7%	$
Northwest	8	24%	$$$
PSA	3	78%	$$$$$
Pan American	6	24%	$$$
Piedmont	3	15%	$$
Southwest	4	0%	$
TWA	8	36%	$$$$
United	15	46%	$$$$$
USAir	5	18%	$$

Note: The more dollar signs, the more expensive the fares are likely to be.

The table makes clear the fact that the larger airlines tend to charge the highest fares. American and United, two of the three airlines with the highest fares, carried more passengers last year than any other airline. On the other hand, Braniff and Midway, two of the three airlines with the lowest fares, carried the smallest number of passengers.

It is important, however, to indicate the limits of these ratings. First, they measure fares only on competitive routes. They do not reflect prices charged on routes dominated by one or two airlines. Second, the ratings reflect different fares between airport pairs, not all fares on all flights. The $200 fare charged by United on ten flights between the same two airports was counted only once. Our statistical analysis shows that counting all fares on all flights would have increased fare differences between the least and most expensive airlines.

Because these fare ratings represent averages for all routes in our sample, they may mask important differences between airline pairs. For example, even though the percentage indexes for TWA and Delta are nearly the same, on shared routes one of these airlines may charge significantly higher fares.

The table below gives fare ratios for airline pairs competing on at least three routes. Each index represents average fares for the first airline divided by average fares for the second one. Ratios less than 1.00 indicate fares on the first airline are less expensive while those above 1.00 are more expensive. For example, the first ratio of 1.06 indicates that, on shared routes, Alaska fares were six percent more expensive than American fares.

The table also includes fare ratings. Plus signs indicate that the first airline offers cheaper fares while minus signs denote that these are more expensive. The more signs, the greater the difference in fares.

FARE COMPARISONS
Carriers Competing on at Least Three Routes

	Fare Ratio	Rating
Alaska/American	1.06	–
Alaska/United	0.97	+
America West/American	0.59	+ + + + +
America West/PSA	0.64	+ + + +
America West/United	0.59	+ + + + +
American/Alaska	0.95	+
American/America West	1.76	– – – – –
American/Braniff	1.86	– – – – –
American/Continental	1.28	– – –

FARE COMPARISONS
Carriers Competing on at Least Three Routes

	Fare Ratio	Rating
American/Delta	1.00	=
American/Eastern	1.18	− −
American/Midway	1.23	− − −
American/Northwest	1.00	=
American/Pan American	1.09	−
American/TWA	1.22	− − −
American/United	1.01	−
American/USAir	1.42	− − − − −
Braniff/American	0.58	+ + + + +
Continental/American	0.80	+ +
Continental/Delta	0.92	+
Continental/Eastern	1.02	−
Continental/Northwest	0.91	+
Continental/Pan American	1.00	=
Continental/TWA	1.12	− −
Continental/United	0.84	+ +
Continental/USAir	1.17	− −
Delta/American	1.00	=
Delta/Continental	1.14	− −
Delta/Eastern	1.00	=
Delta/Northwest	0.96	+
Delta/Pan American	1.08	−
Delta/TWA	1.29	− − −
Delta/United	1.02	−
Eastern/American	0.86	+ +
Eastern/Continental	0.98	+
Eastern/Delta	1.04	−
Eastern/Northwest	0.97	+
Eastern/Pan American	0.94	+
Eastern/TWA	1.19	− −
Eastern/United	0.92	+
Eastern/USAir	1.18	− −
Midway/American	0.82	+ +
Midway/Northwest	0.89	+ +
Midway/TWA	0.83	+ +
Midway/United	0.87	+ +

FARE COMPARISONS
Carriers Competing on at Least Three Routes

	Fare Ratio	Rating
Northwest/American	1.00	=
Northwest/Continental	1.13	– –
Northwest/Delta	1.05	–
Northwest/Eastern	1.04	–
Northwest/Midway	1.13	– –
Northwest/Pan American	1.15	– –
Northwest/Piedmont	1.03	–
Northwest/TWA	1.07	–
Northwest/United	1.00	=
Northwest/USAir	1.04	–
PSA/America West	1.73	– – – – –
PSA/United	1.03	–
Pan American/American	0.93	+
Pan American/Continental	1.03	–
Pan American/Delta	0.93	+
Pan American/Eastern	1.07	–
Pan American/Northwest	0.87	+ +
Pan American/TWA	1.22	– – –
Pan American/United	0.89	+ +
Pan American/USAir	1.21	– – –
Piedmont/Northwest	0.98	+
Piedmont/United	0.88	+ +
Piedmont/USAir	1.02	–
Southwest/United	0.46	+ + + + +
TWA/American	0.88	+ +
TWA/Continental	0.95	+
TWA/Delta	0.82	+ +
TWA/Eastern	0.89	+ +
TWA/Midway	1.21	– – –
TWA/Northwest	0.95	+
TWA/Pan American	0.91	+
TWA/United	0.95	+
TWA/USAir	1.07	–
United/Alaska	1.05	–
United/America West	1.78	– – – – –
United/American	1.01	–

FARE COMPARISONS
Carriers Competing on at Least Three Routes

	Fare Ratio	Rating
United/Continental	1.21	– – –
United/Delta	1.00	=
United/Eastern	1.10	– –
United/Midway	1.17	– –
United/Northwest	1.01	–
United/ PSA	0.97	+
United/Pan American	1.15	– –
United/Piedmont	1.14	– –
United/Southwest	2.19	– – – – –
United/TWA	1.14	– –
United/USAir	1.34	– – – –
USAir/American	0.75	+ + +
USAir/Continental	0.87	+ +
USAir/Eastern	0.87	+ +
USAir/Northwest	0.96	+
USAir/Pan American	0.90	+
USAir/Piedmont	0.98	+
USAir/TWA	0.95	+
USAir/United	0.78	+ + +

2

TRAVEL AGENTS
When and How to Use Them

Travel agencies help plan and make arrangements for trips, including issuing plane tickets. Agencies range from huge national companies like American Express Travel Service and Ask Mr. Foster to one-person firms. Agencies which sell airline tickets must be bonded and meet minimum standards of financial responsibility and professional competence established by either the Airlines Reporting Corporation or the Passenger Network Services Corporation.

In addition to issuing plane tickets, travel agencies can perform a variety of other services related to trips. These include helping you get to and from airports, renting cars, making hotel reservations, and arranging sightseeing tours.

The large majority of all plane tickets are purchased through travel agents. Yet, a significant number (about 30%) are bought by travelers themselves. The following section explains the pros and cons of both options.

SHOULD YOU USE AN AGENT?

The principal benefit of using an agent is convenience. Because travel agents have access to nearly every flight, with one phone call, you can select among several flights. To make your own arrangements, you must call several airlines, select a flight, then call that airline back to reserve or purchase your ticket. Before airline deregulation, more than two phone calls were rarely necessary because airlines were forthcoming with information about the flights of other airlines. But in today's more competitive environment, airlines are often reluctant to supply this information.

A key benefit of using a travel agent is that most do not charge travelers for issuing plane tickets. Instead, airline companies typically pay them 10 percent of the price of the ticket on domestic flights.

Today, a small but increasing number of agents is charging fees, particularly on the purchase of low-price tickets. This practice began in 1985 because deep discounting of tickets substantially reduced agent compensation and because the complexity and variability of fares complicated their job of finding the lowest price.

These charges vary considerably. Often agents charge $5 to $10 for booking an under-$100 ticket or for arranging a ticket refund or reissue. A few base charges on their actual costs of operation, including labor and overhead. Typical transactions can cost from $18 to $30.

Agents who charge for services should not necessarily be avoided. If an agent is charging a $10 fee for low-cost ticketing, regardless of the price of the ticket, there is no motivation to sell you a $140 fare when an $80 fare is available. On the other hand, that same agent selling on a commission basis would lose $6 selling you the $80 ticket instead of the $140 ticket. Also, a few agents that assess fees are willing to rebate the amount of the commission they receive from the airline. Thus, in the example above, the discount fare, plus fee, minus commission, would have come to only $82 ($80 + $10 - $8 = $82).

For several reasons, an agent may not offer you the lowest fare flight, even when you request it. First, because most are paid on commission, the cheaper the flight, the less they make. Because the prices of flights on the same route can vary substantially, an agent may be tempted to secure an average fare, not the lowest one. This is especially true on coast-to-coast flights, where round-trip coach prices can range from $240 to $1000. That's a $76 difference in commission to the agent.

Second, agents may be given special incentives to sell tickets on particular flights. A leading trade journal, for example, has carried ads promising a $100 commission on a $299 flight. On the other hand, a less expensive $200 flight on the same route only offers the agent $20. Incentives from airlines may also take the form of cash bonuses or gifts.

Third, most agents rely heavily on computerized reservation systems that may be biased. Three of the most popular systems are sponsored by individual airlines – Apollo by United, Sabre by American, and PARS by TWA and Northwest. Several years ago, each of these systems was heavily biased in favor of the sponsoring airline. For example, on the Sabre system, American's flights would always be found at the top of the list. More recently, because of the intervention of federal regulators, most of the bias has been removed. Still, other airlines continue to charge that biases remain.

Some travel agencies rely heavily on only one of these systems while others use several, including those independent of any airline. The latter include the Fare Guide, which claims to provide current listings of 24,000 fares between 355 pairs of cities. Some of the larger agencies have developed their own systems, which provide access to several of the other systems. Gelco Travel Services, for instance, claims access not only to all major airline computer systems, but also to information on possible fare and route changes. In the near future, most major systems will offer a software package allowing easy identification of the lowest fare. It pays to find out what systems the agent is using.

Travelers purchasing their own tickets cannot obtain a discount representing the agent's commission unless they belong to groups such as The American Association of Retired Persons and obtain a discount by making a direct purchase.

HOW TO SELECT AN AGENT

If you decide to use an agent to purchase an airline ticket, here are four steps for making the best choice:

1. Ask your friends or business associates for the names of several agencies. For example, the travel agency used by your employer will generally welcome your personal business. If you feel more comfortable doing business in person, make certain the agency is conveniently located.

2. Conduct a phone interview with these agencies. Here are some important questions to ask:

Are you certified? The Institute of Certified Travel Agents certifies agents with at least five year's experience who have completed an extensive travel education program. Called Certified Travel Counsellors, these agents are entitled to use the initials CTC after their names.

How long have you been an agent? Because airline reservation systems are so complex, agents with many years of experience may have learned subtleties about how the airlines operate and how to make this knowledge work for you.

Are you a member of ASTA? The American Society of Travel Agents is the largest and most influential travel agency association in the world. More than half of all U.S. agencies are members. Although ASTA does not aggressively police its members, it does require that they comply with the Society's Principles of Professional Conduct and Ethics. These guidelines prohibit certain unfair practices, such as failing to provide accurate information about services offered or refusing to refund undisputed funds under their control. ASTA has a Consumer Affairs Department which will try to mediate or arbitrate disputes between ASTA member agencies and their customers.

Are you affiliated with larger organizations? Some small- and medium-sized agencies form cooperatives or consortiums to pool information. Because flights and fares have become so complex and changeable, smaller agencies can more easily stay abreast of the latest developments with the assistance of other agencies.

Do you have access to computerized reservation systems? A minority of agencies are still not computerized. They rely on publications, such as the *Official Airline Guide,* and the phone to call for fares. Other agencies have computers but subscribe only to one system, which may be biased. Still others have access to several systems and may even have designed their own. Ask the agency what computer system it uses, if any.

Do you specialize? Like other professionals, many agents specialize. Some primarily serve large institutions while others mainly deal with individuals. The latter are more likely to assist in working out all the details of a trip, including bus, train, car, hotel, and tour reservations. Tell the agents you interview what you are looking for in an agency and ask whether the agency is appropriate for your needs.

3. If you have time, visit the agency in person. Check on the appearance of the office, the number of computer terminals, the number of personnel, and the general attitude of these agents. Because competence and motivation can be judged satisfactorily by the phone interview, this step is the least important of the four.

4. Give the agency a trial. Ask them to make some reservations for you. This will give you an opportunity to evaluate their actual performance. Did the agents treat you politely? Did they seem efficient? Were they knowledgeable? Were there glitches?

One measure of the effectiveness of agents is the kind of questions they ask you. Many will inquire only where you are going and when you want to travel. The best agent will also ask many of the following questions:

- How important is a low fare?
- Can you accept restrictions on changing or cancelling a reservation?
- Which airlines are acceptable? Preferable?
- If a city is served by more than one airport, which ones are acceptable? Preferable?
- Would you like me to make seat reservations? If so, what is your preference?

Instead of specifically asking all of these questions, an effective agent may provide you with options. "There is a TWA flight lasting two hours for $350, and a Piedmont flight lasting three hours for $300. Which do you prefer?"

An effective agent will not hesitate to give advice: "All other factors being equal, fly through Kansas City rather than Chicago because delays are fewer and shorter." "Make certain to arrive at the airport at least 45 minutes before departure because your particular gate is a long walk from the entrance." Some agents will include suggestions like these with the ticket they send you. This is another sign that you have an interested and competent agent.

HOW TO USE AN AGENT EFFECTIVELY

To use agents effectively, give them as much relevant information as possible about your travel needs and preferences. Indicate what is important to you: departure and arrival times, the length of the trip, the route, nonstop versus direct, preferred and unacceptable airlines, preferred and unacceptable airports for departure and landing (if more than one serves an area) and for transfers, the importance of fare, preferred seating, any special dietary needs, and special accommodations for children or the disabled. Since it is unlikely all these factors can be optimized, be prepared to make some trade-offs. The key is to let the agent know the factors that are most important to you.

Finally, do not hesitate to question your agent about the trip. He or she should provide airline and flight number, departure and arrival times, airports, transfers, and fares. Other important questions include:

- Should I call the airline to confirm my flight before leaving for the airport?
- Is the flight likely to be sold out? If so, should I get to the airport a little earlier to confirm my seat?
- What kind of carry-on bags will the plane(s) accommodate? What should I carry on, and what should I check?
- Are any meals served? If so, what type (snack or a hot meal)? Tell the agent about any special dietary needs.

- How far is the walk between planes? Is there transportation? How long will the transfer take?
- What kind of ground transportation will be available at the destination? Do you have any recommendations?

3

FLIGHT SELECTION I
Locating the Most Convenient Flight

For many travelers, convenience is the most important consideration in selecting a flight – when does it leave, how long will it take, are there any stops or plane changes, and, if so, how difficult are the transfers?

If you state specifically what your preferences and constraints are, your travel agent often can do a better job of finding you a convenient flight. The good ones will save you the time and trouble of making a search. Because many agents will not ask for much detail about your needs and preferences, getting what you want requires understanding all the elements that make up convenient flying.

To find the most convenient flight you need to know two things – where information about flights is available, and how this information should be evaluated. Finally, you need to know some basic flight terminology. *Nonstop* flights are just that – you go from point A to B with no stops. *Direct* flights always mean one or more stops – but you do not change planes. *Connection* flight always means that you will have to stop at least once and change planes.

WHERE TO GET INFORMATION

There are three main information sources for flyers who do not wish to rely on an agent – the airlines, private airline flight guides, and computer data bases.

The Airlines: You can obtain information directly from airlines, either by calling on the phone or by visiting an office. They have nearly all the information you need to know. The problem in obtaining information from an airline about their flights is discovering which airlines fly between two areas. You cannot rely on an airline serving a specific route to supply the names of other airlines. They are not required to do so, and you are asking them to provide information potentially harmful to their sales.

One way to obtain this information is to call an airline that you know does not serve the route. Though their representatives might not take the time to list all airlines, they will at least get you some names.

The list below provides an alternative to calling airlines for this information. Check the two states you are flying between and find the names of airlines that serve both. For example, if you wish to travel between Phoenix, Arizona and Little Rock, Arkansas, check with American, Delta, Eastern, Northwest, TWA, and USAir.

Using this list is not foolproof. It does not include small airlines, though many have special agreements with larger ones. In addition, not all major airlines listed serve all cities in a state. However, the list does represent a convenient and useful place to start.

CARRIERS SERVING SPECIFIC STATES	
Who Flies Where?	
Alabama:	American, Delta, Eastern, Northwest, Piedmont, TWA, USAir
Alaska:	Alaska, American, Continental, Delta, Hawaiian, Northwest, TWA, United
Arizona:	Alaska, American, America West, Braniff, Continental, Delta, Eastern, Midwest, Northwest, PSA, TWA, United, USAir

CARRIERS SERVING SPECIFIC STATES
Who Flies Where?

Arkansas:	American, Delta, Northwest, TWA, United
California:	Alaska, American, America West, Braniff, Continental, Delta, Eastern, Hawaiian, Northwest, PSA, Pan Am, Piedmont, TWA, United, USAir
Colorado:	American, America West, Continental, Delta, Eastern, Midwest, Northwest, Piedmont, TWA, United, USAir
Connecticut:	America West, Continental, Delta, Eastern, Northwest, Pan Am, Piedmont, TWA, United, USAir
Delaware:	Eastern, Northwest, United, USAir
Dist. of Columbia:	Alaska, American, Braniff, Continental, Delta, Eastern, Midwest, Northwest, Pan Am, Piedmont, TWA, United, USAir
Florida:	American, Braniff, Continental, Delta, Eastern, Midwest, Northwest, Pan Am, Piedmont, TWA, United, USAir
Georgia:	American, Continental, Delta, Eastern, Northwest, Pan Am, Piedmont, TWA, United
Hawaii:	American, Continental, Delta, Hawaiian, Northwest, Pan Am, TWA, United
Idaho:	Alaska, Delta, TWA, United

CARRIERS SERVING SPECIFIC STATES
Who Flies Where?

Illinois:	Alaska, American, America West, Braniff, Continental, Delta, Eastern, Midwest, Northwest, Pan Am, Piedmont, TWA, United, USAir
Indiana:	American, Continental, Delta, Eastern, Midwest, Northwest, Pan Am, Piedmont, TWA, United, USAir
Iowa:	American, America West, Continental, Midway, Northwest, TWA, United
Kansas:	American, America West, Northwest, TWA, United
Kentucky:	American, Continental, Delta, Eastern, Piedmont, TWA, United, USAir
Louisiana:	American, Continental, Delta, Eastern, Midwest, Northwest, Piedmont, TWA, United, USAir
Maine:	Continental, Delta, United
Maryland:	American, America West, Braniff, Continental, Delta, Northwest, Piedmont, TWA, United, USAir
Massachusetts:	American, Braniff, Continental, Delta, Eastern, Midwest, Northwest, Pan Am, Piedmont, TWA, United, USAir
Michigan:	American, Braniff, Continental, Delta, Eastern, Midwest, Northwest, Pan Am, Piedmont, TWA, United, USAir

CARRIERS SERVING SPECIFIC STATES
Who Flies Where?

Minnesota:	American, Continental, Delta, Eastern, Midwest, Northwest, Pan Am, Piedmont, TWA, United
Mississippi:	American, Continental, Delta, Eastern, Northwest, United
Missouri:	American, America West, Braniff, Continental, Delta, Eastern, Midwest, Northwest, Piedmont, TWA, United
Montana:	Continental, Delta, Northwest, United
Nebraska:	American, America West, Delta, Northwest, TWA, United
Nevada:	Alaska, American, America West, Braniff, Continental, Delta, Eastern, Hawaiian, Midwest, Northwest, PSA, TWA, United, USAir
New Hampshire:	Continental, United, USAir
New Jersey:	American, Continental, Eastern, Northwest, Piedmont, TWA, United, USAir
New Mexico:	American, America West, Continental, Delta, Eastern, PSA, TWA, United, USAir
New York:	American, America West, Braniff, Continental, Delta, Eastern, Midwest, Pan Am, Piedmont, TWA, United, USAir
North Carolina:	American, Continental, Delta, Eastern, Pan Am, Piedmont, TWA, United, USAir

CARRIERS SERVING SPECIFIC STATES
Who Flies Where?

North Dakota:	Continental, Delta, Northwest, United
Ohio:	American, Continental, Delta, Eastern, Midwest, Northwest, Pan Am, Piedmont, TWA, United, USAir
Oklahoma:	American, Continental, Delta, Eastern, Northwest, TWA, United
Oregon:	Alaska, American, America West, Continental, Delta, Eastern, Hawaiian, Northwest, PSA, TWA, United
Pennsylvania:	American, Continental, Delta, Eastern, Midwest, Northwest, Piedmont, TWA, United, USAir
Rhode Island:	American, Continental, Eastern, Northwest, Pan Am, Piedmont, TWA, United, USAir
South Carolina:	American, Continental, Delta, Eastern, Piedmont, United, USAir
South Dakota:	Continental, Delta, Northwest, TWA, United
Tennessee:	American, Continental, Delta, Eastern, Northwest, Pan Am, Piedmont, TWA, United, USAir
Texas:	Alaska, American, America West, Braniff, Continental, Delta, Eastern, Midwest, Northwest, Pan Am, Piedmont, TWA, United, USAir

CARRIERS SERVING SPECIFIC STATES
Who Flies Where?

Utah:	American, America West, Continental, Delta, Eastern, Northwest, Pan Am, United
Vermont:	Continental, Piedmont, United, USAir
Virginia:	American, Braniff, Continental, Delta, Eastern, Piedmont, TWA, United, USAir
Washington:	Alaska, American, America West, Braniff, Continental, Delta, Eastern, Hawaiian, Northwest, PSA, Pan Am, Piedmont, TWA, United
West Virginia:	Continental, Piedmont, TWA, United, USAir
Wisconsin:	American, Continental, Eastern, Northwest, TWA, United, USAir
Wyoming:	Delta, Northwest, United

Airline Guides: The most popular publication listing most flights in North America is called the *Official Airline Guide: North American Edition*. This extremely useful guide comes in a desk edition and a much smaller pocket edition.

The larger edition is a telephone book sized paperback published twice a month. It contains information on 74,100 direct flights and about 200,000 flights with connections between 34,000 pairs of cities. The smaller pocket edition is approximately 400 pages and is published once a month in paperback. It lists 55,000 direct flights between 7,355 pairs of cities. The smaller guide provides all the non-stop and direct flights between the cities listed.

A current edition of either of these contains much of the flight information, but not fares, available to a travel agent. Travelers who prefer to make their own decisions about times, connections, and even meals may prefer to consult the *OAG* rather than an agent. But keep in mind that this publication has a 40-day lead time, so it may contain outdated information.

For each flight, the guides list the following information:

- Day(s) of week the flight operates
- Times of all departures and arrivals, including connections
- Airports of departure, arrival, and any connections
- Airline and flight number
- Classes of service
- Meal service, if any – breakfast, dinner, lunch, snack

These publications are available in many libraries or can be purchased by calling 1-800-323-3537 or 1-800-942-1888 (Illinois). Single copies of the desk top edition cost $30, the pocket guide $10. The guides do not contain fares, but these are available in an *OAG* supplement costing $50.

Computer Data Bases: If you have a home computer with a telephone modem, you can tap into a number of computer data bases for information on flights, hotels, rental cars, entertainment, and restaurants. Some computer airline systems permit users to become their own travel agents, booking flights themselves. (You will not, however, qualify for the agent's commission.) Deregulation of the travel agent industry may produce new travel-related data bases, and the number of computer owners who use their computers to obtain travel information could increase sharply.

Although computer systems charge users for connection time, they may offer some advantages over using certain travel agents. You can obtain travel information on nights and weekends, and the companies claim that their information is more complete, more timely, and less biased than airline data or information from some travel agents. On the other hand, there are times when only travel agents can have certain fare restrictions lifted.

The two major computer airline reservations programs are offered by the *Official Airline Guide* and by *ABC Travel Guides*. In addition, subscribers to CompuServe and other on-line information sources can gain access to the various airline computer systems. Each program keeps tabs on 100,000 schedule changes and maintains information on 1,750,000 different flights. They also list fares. With these systems, you tell the computer where you want to go, from which airport, and roughly when. They will then display relevant timetable information. You can also inquire about fares and receive a complete spread of fares available on a preferred route and any conditions that apply to them.

Computer electronic versions of the *Official Airline Guide* for flight information are available for a one-time, $50 subscription fee and user charge averaging $3 a transaction. Dunn and Bradstreet says its electronic computer access system versions of the *OAG* are more current than regular *OAG* books because domestic fares are updated daily and all flight schedules are updated weekly rather than twice monthly. The computer access system versions contain airfares and claim to give equal treatment to the more than 700 airlines on the system. By contrast, reservation systems used by some travel agents and airlines do not include all airlines and may be biased toward one airline.

HOW TO ASSESS CONVENIENCE

For most travelers, the time period when you can travel and total flight time are the two most important convenience factors. In addition, the time you choose to travel can have a direct impact on whether your plane will be on time. This is information most readily available from agents, airlines, and the airline guides.

When You Travel: If you are traveling for business, you will probably have some severe time constraints. However, if you have any flexibility regarding time, consider that some periods of the day are far better for air travel than are others. Most important, try to avoid flights departing or arriving before 10 a.m. or between 5 and 8 p.m. During these peak periods, airports will be most crowded and flight delays most frequent. (Also, fares may be lower during non-peak travel times.)

Flight Time: Total flight time will always be shortest on nonstop flights. Making a stop will usually add at least 45 minutes, and often longer, to a trip. If a stop is necessary, it usually takes less time on a direct flight — one where you stay on the same plane — than on a connecting flight. Moreover, you will avoid the inconvenience of changing planes and minimize the chance of losing any checked luggage.

If a transfer is required, however, staying with the same airline is usually more convenient than shifting to another airline. Even if the time delay before the second flight is the same for both airlines, sticking with the one that brought you has two convenience advantages: the gates are usually closer; and the airline is more likely to accommodate any delay in your first flight by moving back the departure time of the second flight. Of course, there are exceptions. On a recent Northwest flight from Washington to Milwaukee with a change of planes in Detroit, we landed at the Detroit airport, then were held on the tarmac for 30 minutes, and finally were taken to the gate that had first been vacated by our connecting flight to Milwaukee.

Here are some other important factors that affect convenience:

Location of Airports: When you can choose between two or three airports, consider the time it takes to get to each from your home or business. This is a choice that travelers to cities such as New York (Kennedy, LaGuardia, Newark, White Plains), Washington, D.C. (National, Dulles, Baltimore/Washington), Chicago (O'Hare, Midway), Houston (Houston International, Hobby), and Los Angeles (LAX, Burbank, Ontario, Long Beach) may have to make.

Adequacy of Parking: If you drive to the airport, consider the location of parking areas, the likelihood of their being filled, and the regularity of shuttle transport between these areas and the terminals. For example, Washington National's close-in lots are generally full by mid-morning on a weekday. This forces the use of satellite parking, which is poorly served by shuttle service. Close-in lots are usually open in the early morning or in the evening.

Long Lines at Ticket Counters: These can be avoided by purchasing your tickets in advance and by using luggage that can be carried on the plane. If you do both, when you get to the airport you can proceed directly to the gate.

Location of Gates: The gates of some airlines may be much more conveniently located than are others. This tends to be a more important consideration at older airports with long piers. Travel agents can be helpful in assessing this factor. As a general rule, the more conveniently located gates are used by major airlines for popular flights. Yet, be forewarned that there are numerous exceptions to this rule.

Multi-Stops: The more stops your flight makes, the greater likelihood of delays. Thus, nonstop flights are shortest not just because of the time a stopover takes, but also because there are fewer chances for a delay. Delays are especially frequent at hub airports, where a large number of flights by the same airline are often scheduled at or near the same time. Information on the frequency of delays experienced by different airlines can be found in the chapter on flight problems.

Long Walks to Connecting Flights: Passengers can walk nearly a mile to transfer from Continental to Aspen Air flights in Denver, Colorado, for example. Similar distances can be found at O'Hare and at Detroit. In general, one is more likely to be forced to walk long distances between planes at older, large airports, such as Denver, O'Hare, St. Louis, and Detroit. Newer airports, such as Houston International, Dallas/Ft. Worth, and Atlanta, run small rail cars between terminals or piers. Taking nonstop or direct flights will avoid most of these problems. If you must transfer planes, consult travel agents or airlines about ways to minimize any difficulties.

Long Waits for Luggage: Traveling light and carrying your luggage on the plane is the best way to avoid this inevitable problem.

4

FLIGHT SELECTION II
Finding the Least Expensive Fare

For most travelers making personal (non-business) trips, finding a low fare is a top priority. The good news is that airline deregulation has spawned some incredibly low fares. In 1986, for example, you could fly one-way between Denver and Colorado Springs for $9, between New York and Florida for $49, and between New York and Los Angeles for $99. While fares have risen recently, some terrific bargains are still available.

The bad news is that these low-priced fares are difficult to find because: so many fares are offered, they can change rapidly, and they are sometimes hidden by airlines or agents. It is not unusual for a computer listing of fares between large cities to show more than 100 different rates, which can differ quite substantially. In late 1985, round-trip coach fares between New York and Miami ranged from $118 to $646. Even on one airline, the differences can be huge. In early 1986, American's round-trip coach fares between Chicago and Long Beach, California ranged from $238 to $800. In late 1985, Eastern's one-way rates between Baltimore/Washington and Boston varied from $39 to $210.

Fares change much more frequently now than before deregulation, and sometimes with astonishing speed. In the first half of 1986, for instance, Frontier lowered its Denver-Chicago coach fare from $120 to $89, hiked it to $109, reduced it to $79, and raised it back to $109.

Low fares are sometimes hidden by airlines and not aggressively sought by travel agents. Why? There are several reasons. It often does not pay to advertise rates that change rapidly or are offered on only a limited number of seats on a flight. Moreover, passengers paying higher fares, full coach or first class, may resent reading in newspapers that their seats are being sold at half the price they paid.

As explained in an earlier chapter, travel agents are faced with a dilemma. Most would like to help find the lowest fares possible for travelers who request them. Yet, unless they charge fees, in doing so they pay a price. Since agents receive a percentage commission based on fares, the lower the rate, the lower the compensation. Furthermore, lower rates often require the most time to locate and book. Still, in order to satisfy customers and build their business, many agents will look hard for the best deal – a low fare plus convenience.

WHY FARES DIFFER

Understanding which factors influence fares can help you find low priced tickets. Here are some considerations that will influence the cost of your ticket.

Seating: Traditionally, first-class fares have been 20 to 50 percent higher than full, undiscounted coach rates. But the spread of discount coach fares has widened the ticket price gap between the two classes. In late 1985, for example, Delta charged $840 for a first-class ticket and $646 for an unrestricted coach ticket on a round-trip flight between Miami/Ft. Lauderdale and New York but also offered coach fares of $238, $198, $179, and $138. In the same period, United charged $300 for a first-class ticket and $188 for an unrestricted coach ticket on a round-trip flight between San Francisco and Los Angeles yet also offered coach fares of $148, $118, and $98.

Because of the increased reluctance of flyers to pay the full first-class fare, some airlines have introduced a business class with fares between those of first class and coach. Business class service often comes with wider-than coach seats and free drinks.

Airlines: On average, major airlines like United and American charge higher fares than cut-rate airlines like Continental. But all airlines offer such a variety of fares on particular routes that one cannot be sure that the lowest fare is on the discounters.

Both these points are illustrated by the following list of one-way air fares from Washington, National to Boston and New York City in late 1985. Paired fares represent the highest and lowest.

ONE-WAY FARES **from Washington National to...**		
	Boston	New York
American	N/A	$109/99
Delta	$179/80	$119/95
Eastern	$179/80	$75/50
New York Air	$115/80	$75/50
People Express	$89/59	$59/39
USAir	$75/39	$96/83

On these routes, American, Delta, and Eastern tended to charge higher fares than the other airlines, and on average, the late People Express charged the least.

Still, it is important to note that to Boston, fares were lower on USAir than on People Express. In fact, frequently the lowest fare charged by the major airlines was lower than the highest fare offered by People. Recent mergers eliminating discount airlines like People may well diminish the variation in rates among airlines.

Advance Purchase: Many airlines now offer discounts on tickets purchased 3, 7, 14, 21, or 30 days before the flight. As a general rule, the earlier the purchase, the lower the fare. On round-trip flights between Los Angeles and San Francisco in late 1985, for example, both AirCal and PSA charged coach fares of $98/118 with a 3-day advance purchase, $125 with a 14-day advance purchase, and $148/188 with no advance purchase.

The risk here is not being able to use the ticket and then being charged a cancellation fee. And these fees are increasing. This past year, for example, American hiked its cancellation fees from 25 percent to 50 percent on 30-day advance-purchase fares and imposed a 25 percent fee on 21-day advance purchase, and a 10 percent fee on a 7-day and 14-day advance-purchase fares. This penalty usually is assessed even if you switch to another flight on the same airline.

Because of the 50 percent penalty, on 30-day advance purchase you should be pretty certain that you will be able to take advantage of the roughly 70 percent discount off full fare. It may make more sense to buy the 21-day advance-purchase ticket since this fare is discounted nearly as much (65 percent) yet is subject only to a 25 percent penalty.

Time of Flights: Sometimes these advance-purchase discounts can be obtained only if you agree to fly on certain days and sometimes at certain hours on one of these days. Typically, travelers have to stay over a Saturday night.

There are several other types of time restrictions. In the past, on certain advance-purchase tickets American has charged lower fares for travel on Tuesday and Wednesday. On New York to Miami flights, Eastern's discount days are Monday through Thursday. Yet, many airlines reserve their lowest fares for weekend flights.

Perhaps the best known time discount is available on midnight flights. In late 1985, for instance, one airline charged a regular round-trip coach fare of $188 between Los Angeles and San Francisco, but only $78 for their midnight flight.

Nonrefundable Purchase: This year, many airlines are offering nonrefundable tickets called maxsavers. These fares may cost as little as 20 percent of regular coach fares. Most airlines restrict maxsavers to popular routes and require a two-day advance purchase and Saturday-night stay.

There are exceptions to the nonrefundability rule. All airlines issue refunds if the airport is closed because of bad weather or if a flight is cancelled. Most airlines will also make refunds to travelers who miss a flight because of illness or death in the immediate family. The airlines will also waive any penalties if you have to reschedule under these circumstances. You must provide written proof, such as a letter from your doctor or funeral director. Lastly, most airlines allow ticket holders who miss their flight, but arrive within two hours of departure, to fly standby on the next available flight.

Capacity Controlling: Increasingly, on any given flight, airlines offer only a limited number of seats at a discount fare. The number of these seats (called "capacity-controlled") can vary from flight to flight and from day to day. But they are available only until sold out. And the number of capacity-controlled seats is by no means standard. They can be available six weeks before the flight or six hours. In addition, the number may be reduced or increased depending on marketplace conditions.

For example, a CBS News report by Betsy Ashton recently uncovered the following practice between two airlines flying between the same cities. Because each airline company had access to the reservation systems of the others, it was easy for them to check on the competition. When the seats on the first airline were sold out, the second airline company immediately cancelled all their low-priced seats, even though some were still available, because they realized the consumer had nowhere else to go for a ticket.

The discounts on these fares are usually less than on advance-purchase fares, but not always. And they nearly always represent a substantial savings off full fares. These two points are illustrated by past fares between San Francisco and Los Angeles. Capacity-controlled fares on both AirCal and PSA were as low as $90 (compared to $188 full-fare), whereas the 14-day advance-purchase ticket cost $125. Furthermore, the former were not subject to cancellation fees.

Airports: If you are going to or coming from a city with two or more airports, choosing the right airport can save you money. For example, the following table lists highest and lowest fares from Washington-area airports to Boston by different airlines in late 1985. While two of the four airlines using both airports charged the same fares, the other two did not.

HIGHEST AND LOWEST FARES to Boston from Washington		
	National	Dulles
Eastern	$179/80	$179/80
New York Air	115/80	75/39
People Express	89/59	55/35
USAir	75/39	75/39

Nonstop vs. Transfer Flights: On lengthy trips, it is often cheaper to take a flight requiring a connection than to fly nonstop or direct. Airlines offer these lower transfer fares, which appear to be about 10 to 25 percent lower than nonstop fares, to compensate for the greater inconvenience of changing planes. Be aware, however, that this will increase your chances of a delay.

Point-Beyond: One result of deregulation is that fares today often reflect marketing programs and popularity more than distance traveled. In fact, many times, a longer connecting flight will cost less than shorter flights to the point of connection. For example, coast-to-coast flights from New York to Los Angeles stopping in Chicago can cost less than certain flights between New York and Chicago. Flights between Kansas City and Houston that stop in Dallas have been $100 cheaper than flights from Kansas City to Dallas.

As a result, experienced travelers will often book a connecting flight from New York to Los Angeles, but simply get off in Chicago. Two cautions, however: make certain to carry on all luggage so that it does not travel to the point beyond; and check to see that because you fail to show up for the second leg of your trip, the airline doesn't cancel your return.

Tour-Based Fares: Some computer listings include fares which are tour-based (IT). Tour-based rates are lower than full coach fares. Several years ago, for example, the roundtrip tour fare between Dallas and Denver was $229 while the coach price was $444. To qualify for these fares, you must participate in the tour. Beware: such a tour may require you to pay for hotel accommodations, a rental car, or theater tickets. In fact, tour-based rates are rarely the least expensive fares available.

FARES FOR SPECIAL GROUPS

Members of certain groups sometimes qualify for discounts.

Children: All major airlines allow children under two years of age held by a parent to ride free. They also offer discounts of 20 to 25 percent off the adult fare to children under 12 riding in their own seat, unless the fare is already a deep discount.

Ministers and Military: A few airlines also offer discounts to clergy and armed service personnel. Members of these two groups should ask travel agents or airlines about special rates.

Seniors: In 1985, American began offering to senior citizens a 10 percent discount on all flights. These reductions could even be taken on advance-purchase and other discount fares. By 1987, nearly all major airlines had their own special fares for seniors. Most offered a ten percent discount for those 65 and over with no restrictions on flights. Braniff, however, granted a 15 percent discount. Both Delta and Eastern sold booklets of four or eight discount tickets with certain flight restrictions. Eastern also offered the 10 percent discount. Listed below are the principal features of senior fares offered by major airlines in early 1987.

Eastern and TWA offered fixed-price passes allowing travel anywhere in the U.S. for a year. The Eastern "Get-Up and Go" Passport, costing $1299 in early 1987, could be used for up to one trip a week. Those 62 and older were eligible.

TWA's VSP Senior Pass, selling for $1399, could be used as frequently as desired. But no more than three flights on the same route could be taken, travel in certain holiday periods was blocked, and reservations had to be made 7 to 21 days in advance. Eligibility began at age 65.

DISCOUNTS FOR SENIORS

Airline	Discount	Age Eligible	Fee	Flight Restrictions
American	10%	65	$25/year	None
Braniff	15%	65	None	None
Cont/NY Air	10%	65	$25/life	None
Delta	TB[1]	62	None	Yes[2]
Eastern A	10%	65	$25/year	None
Eastern B	TB[1]	62	None	Yes[3]
Pan American	40%	65	None	Yes[4]
Piedmont	10%	65	$25/life	None
TWA	10%	62	$25/life	None
United	10%	65	$25/year	None

1. TB = Ticket Book — Four one-way tickets for $87 each, or eight tickets for $74 each.
2. No reservations can be made until six days before flight Tuesday-Thursday and Saturday.
3. Not on Sunday, Friday, before noon on Monday, and after noon on Thursday.
4. Only NYC-DC Shuttle at certain times

HOW TO FIND LOW FARES

There are four main sources of information about low fares.

Ads: Sometimes the cheapest fares are advertised by airlines in newspapers and magazines. But these are usually fares on frequently traveled routes, and they often are not available when you want to travel.

Agents: As already mentioned, because of the time they must spend and the prospect of a reduced commission, some travel agents will not enthusiastically search for the lowest fare. Yet, others who are trying to cultivate your business, or who are just trying to be helpful, are willing to make this effort. Keep in mind it may well be worth paying them a fee for this service.

Airlines: Calling all the airlines that serve a particular route does not guarantee finding the cheapest fare. Reservation agents will rarely volunteer information about special group rates, tour-based fares, or point-beyond prices, for example. They may even neglect to mention capacity-controlled fares. But if you stress the importance of a low fare, in all likelihood your calls will turn up at least one significant discount, particularly if you call at least two weeks before the flight.

Computer Data Bases: With a home computer, you can access fares as well as airline schedules. Electronic versions of the *Official Airline Guide* not only contain fare listings, but also are more current than *OAG* publications because domestic fares are updated daily. The *OAG* lists fares from low to high so you can choose the least expensive at a glance. Only fares that match your travel day, date, time, and length of stay are displayed. Schedules and fares are linked so you can easily find the fare corresponding to a schedule, or vice versa. The *OAG* access program can be accessed for a one-time subscriber fee of $50 and per-transaction costs of about $3.

Those with a computer can also subscribe to CompuServe,

which offers access to the TWA reservations system, Pan Am's *Travel Guide*, and the electronic *OAG*. Each program contains information on fares. To connect with CompuServe, the cost is $12.50/hour on weekdays and $6/hour evenings and weekends. Hourly charges for reservations and booking are higher.

5

RESERVATIONS AND TICKETING

How to Reserve Seats, Purchase Tickets, and Obtain Refunds

Many travelers purchase a ticket at the same time they make reservations. Others, however, make reservations well in advance but wait until the advance-purchase deadline or the day of the flight to buy the ticket. This chapter evaluates both of these strategies, explains how to obtain refunds on cancelled or lost tickets, and offers tips on coping with airline over-booking and bankruptcy.

HOW TO MAKE RESERVATIONS

Reserving a seat on a flight sometime before purchasing a ticket has an important advantage — you are virtually guaranteed a seat on the flight but are under no obligation to buy a ticket, even if you forget to cancel the reservation. The one condition you must meet is to make the purchase by the time stipulated by the airline. This is usually an hour before the flight on non-advance-purchase fares. Note, however, that you will be charged the fare offered at the time of purchase, not at the time of reservation.

Perhaps the most important thing to remember about reservations is to make them early. This is especially true for flights during busy holiday seasons. Yet, it is increasingly important for all trips. Airlines have responded to deregulation by trying to fill more seats on all their flights. And they are succeeding. The chances of being able to make a reservation with less than a day's notice are far less today than several years ago. There are two basic ways individuals can make reservations.

By Phone: Most reservations made by individuals are made by a direct phone call to the airline. The most important thing you should remember, after making the reservation, is to review all important information with the airline representative. This information includes spelling of your name, flight numbers, departure and arrival times and airports, the fare amount, and any restrictions or cancellation penalties. The latter is especially important when receiving an advance-purchase discount.

By Computer: Travelers with a personal computer and modem (which allows communication with other computers through phone lines) can also make reservations through access systems offered by several companies. TWA makes available a Travel Shopper reservation system activated by a user identification code it supplies. Users may make reservations on all major U.S. airlines except United and Southwest. They are billed $21 or $32.50 an hour, depending on the time of day. American's Sabre system and the *Official Airline Guide Electronic Edition* also offer the opportunity to make reservations in addition to the ability to access flight information.

Few travelers currently use their computer to make reservations because they do not have the necessary equipment. Even more importantly, using these systems is time-consuming and expensive. The research and screen-scrolling involved in selecting a flight may take as long as 30 minutes. This would cost at least $10 and possibly more than $15. Calling airlines or travel agents is usually easier, and certainly cheaper, though it may not be less time-consuming.

HOW TO PURCHASE A TICKET

Tickets can be purchased through a travel agent, over the phone, at an airline office, at an airport ticket counter, at an automated ticket machine, or by personal computer. No matter what the method of purchase, ticket prices are usually the same. Moreover, once a ticket has been purchased, the fare is guaranteed. It cannot be increased by the airline between the time of purchase and the flight.

Through an Agent: Travel agents will, if there is sufficient time, mail tickets to you or allow you to pick them up at their offices. Some will even deliver them. They will accept cash or a check but may delay giving you tickets until the latter has cleared. Most will not accept purchase by credit card over the phone unless you are a regular customer.

By Phone: All major airlines allow the purchase of tickets by phone with a credit card. They will always accept American Express, Diners Club, Mastercard, or VISA, and sometimes other cards. Airlines may agree to mail out the tickets less than a week before the flight. But we advise allowing this mailing only when there is at least two weeks leeway. If a ticket is delayed or lost in the mails, the airline may require you to repurchase the ticket, then apply for a refund. We know of one case where a flyer purchased a Northwest ticket over the phone a week before departure. It was mailed but did not arrive in time for the flight, and Northwest forced the consumer to purchase a second ticket. If you are nervous about the mail, you should pick up the ticket at a travel agency, ticket office, or airport ticket counter.

There usually is no special fee for most credit card purchases by phone. The exception is credit card purchase of a ticket for someone else who picks up the ticket at the airport. Most airlines assess a fee of around $15 to $20. This "prepaid fee" can be avoided if the ticket is mailed to the person using it.

At an Airline Office: Most major airlines have offices

in large cities, often in downtown hotels. These offices, which are usually more convenient than airports, make reservations and sell tickets. They accept cash, major credit cards, and checks with two major IDs (driver's license, major credit card, employee card).

At an Airport Ticket Counter: Of course, tickets can be purchased at airport ticket counters. But this should be avoided because lines can be long and slow, and not all airlines will inquire if anyone in line has a reservation on a flight about to take off. You should arrive at least 45 minutes before flight time to purchase a ticket. Except on shuttle flights, no airline of which we are aware sells tickets, even to those with reservations, at the gate or on the plane.

Another reason to avoid purchasing your ticket at the airport is that you may have a poor selection of seats. Since many fliers now select their seats when they purchase their tickets, waiting to purchase at the airport will often leave you with just middle seats or those near the smoking section.

Automatic Ticket Machine: For several years, some travelers have been able to bypass long lines at airport ticket counters by purchasing tickets from automatic ticket machines (ATMs). Recently, airlines like American have placed these machines in many downtown ticket offices as well, where in some cases they are available 24 hours a day. Although these ATMs can be convenient to use, they have their limitations. They sell tickets for flights on just one airline. These flights may be limited to certain high-volume routes. The machines may not offer most discount fares, and they may not accept all major credit cards.

Yet, as the machines are improved, these limitations are lessening. The newest generation of ATM makes reservations, issues tickets and boarding passes, makes seat assignments, and updates your frequent flyer account. A machine that permits ticket purchases on more than one airline is being developed.

By Computer: The computer data bases that allow reservations also permit ticket purchases with a credit card. At present, however, the tickets must be mailed from the airline, picked up at the ticket office, or obtained from an agent.

Wherever you buy your ticket, check to make certain it contains correct information. Most important is the "status" box. If it does not say "OK," your flight is not confirmed.

COPING WITH OVER-BOOKING

Because many individuals making reservations do not end up purchasing tickets, airlines routinely try to over-book flights, on average by about 20 percent. The number of no-shows is so large – seven million at American last year – most people with reservations are able to get on their flights. But a minority cannot – in 1986, about 200,000 on all airlines.

Most airlines offer inducements to persuade passengers to be voluntarily bumped. Typically, these take the form of a round trip plane ticket to anywhere the airline flies in the U.S., in addition to a space on the next flight to your immediate destination. Consequently, more than 70 percent of those bumped last year were volunteers.

If, however, there are not enough volunteers, passengers can be involuntarily bumped. Usually this is done in the reverse order of check-in, so that the last to arrive are the first to be bumped. If the airline can arrange to get passengers to their final destinations within an hour of the scheduled arrival of the original flight, there is no compensation. However, if the delay is any longer, the airline must also pay a penalty, in addition to getting the flyer to his/her destination, or refund the ticket. If the second flight arrives between one and two hours after the original flight, this compensation is the price of the ticket up to $200. If the arrival is delayed more than two hours, the penalty is twice the price of the ticket up to $400. This rule, though, applies only to flights on planes with at least 60 seats.

Should you ever volunteer for bumping? That depends on

whether you can afford the time delay and whether the compensation is adequate. If it is an airline ticket, does it require you to fly standby? In what period of time must it be used? Does it cover routes you wish to fly? Furthermore, if the airline cannot arrange another flight leaving shortly, will it pay for a meal, for telephone calls, or, if you are forced to stay overnight, for a hotel room?

HOW TO OBTAIN A REFUND ON CANCELLED OR LOST TICKETS

Except on tickets with special restrictions, airlines provide refunds when reservations are cancelled. If more than one airline is involved, these are usually supplied by the one issuing the ticket. Refunds generally take the same form as the payment — cash, check, or credit card credit. You should be aware that on a cancelled ticket purchased with a credit card, federal law requires airlines to provide a credit within seven days of the cancellation. DOT, however, has received many complaints recently that airlines, especially Continental, have ignored this law.

It is far more difficult, time-consuming, and possibly expensive to obtain refunds on lost or stolen tickets than on cancelled ones. Airlines explain that this is because tickets are easily used on another flight or, if purchased with cash, converted back to cash. Most importantly, contact the airline issuing the tickets immediately because some airlines have time limits on refunds of lost tickets and because, if the tickets are used, you'll receive no refunds. Then be prepared to wait for at least 120 days and possibly to pay a fee, typically $20 to $35, before receiving the refund.

COPING WITH AIRLINE BANKRUPTCY

A minor risk of purchasing a ticket well in advance is that the airline will go bankrupt and other airlines will not accept the ticket. The risk is small because few airlines go out of business. Those that do are usually taken over by other airlines which honor the tickets. Yet, the risk does exist. For example, when Continental filed for bankruptcy in 1983, other airlines refused to honor its tickets.

There are three strategies you can pursue to minimize or eliminate this risk. You can reserve tickets well in advance but purchase them shortly before the flight. The disadvantage here is that you cannot qualify for advance-purchase discount fares. A better strategy is to use a credit card to purchase tickets using a credit card from an issuer that, in the event of bankruptcy, will credit your account for the amount of the fare. American Express, for instance, advertises a default protection plan. A third option is to purchase default protection insurance. While this insurance would provide compensation, it is very expensive — typically $5.50 or $6 for $100 of protection. We do not recommend that consumers purchase it unless they wish to take advantage of deep discounts for advance purchase on financially unstable airlines.

RATING THE AIRLINES

In 1986 and the first half of 1987, DOT received thousands of complaints about reservations, ticketing, oversales, and boarding problems. These grievances are related to airline or travel agent mistakes, problems making reservations or obtaining tickets, busy reservation phone lines, delays in mailing tickets, or problems boarding the aircraft, including oversales. Listed below are complaint rates and summary evaluations for individual airlines. Note that Delta, American, and Piedmont are the major airlines with *good* or *very good* ratings, while Continental, Pan American, and TWA are large airlines with *poor* or *very poor* evaluations.

CONSUMER COMPLAINTS
Reservations, Ticketing Oversales, and Boarding

Airline	Complaints per 100,000 Passengers	Evaluation
Alaska	0.07	Very Good
America West	0.34	Fair
American	0.23	Good
Braniff	0.55	Fair
Continental	1.96	Very Poor
Delta	0.12	Very Good
Eastern	0.41	Fair
Hawaiian	0.88	Poor
Midway	0.30	Fair
Northwest	0.56	Fair
PSA	0.19	Good
Pan American	1.03	Very Poor
Piedmont	0.22	Good
Southwest	0.11	Very Good
TWA	0.71	Poor
United	0.42	Fair
USAir	0.29	Fair

6

FREQUENT FLYER PROGRAMS
When and How to Use Them

Frequent flyer programs have become extremely popular with many travelers. The 10 million Americans enrolled in these programs get credit, usually in the form of miles, for every mile they fly. When certain totals are reached, the flyer can turn them in for free flights or for other awards. Many travelers use these "points" to fly first class on coach tickets.

This chapter describes these programs, explains how to participate, and lists the pros and cons of frequent flyer programs.

SHOULD YOU JOIN?

Frequent flyer programs offer premiums ranging from two first-class tickets around the world with hotel and rental cars to an upgrade to first class. But along with these attractive benefits, there are costs and limits to be weighed. First of all, there is the time it takes to fill out applications when required, monitor your accounts, and make sure you receive credit for your flights. Second, you may pay higher fares and suffer greater inconvenience to "build up miles." And finally, after patiently building up mileage, you may find that the premiums are, for practical purposes, not available to you.

Some airlines place ceilings on the number of seats available to frequent flyers on popular routes (e.g., Hawaii and Mexico). Others have begun to declare blackout days prohibiting travel on frequent flyer mileage. In particular, traveling during holidays or the summer may be difficult on frequent flyer programs.

Should you, then, participate in frequent flyer programs? If you don't fly often over lengthy distances, you may never qualify for any substantial award. As a result, signing up may be more trouble than it's worth.

If you do log many miles each year, we suggest pursuing one of two strategies. First, if the awards are not that important to you, just sign up for programs with airlines you frequently fly, then forget about them. These airlines will periodically mail you a record of mileage. You can then check to see if you've qualified for any good trips.

Second, if you're deadly serious about piling up frequent flyer mileage and winning particular awards, sign up for a limited number of programs, then make every effort to travel on these airlines. This strategy makes the most sense if someone else is paying for your tickets.

HOW TO PARTICIPATE

All frequent flyer programs can be joined by completing an application available at travel agencies, ticket offices, airport ticket counters, or even on planes. Some airlines do not even require an application but will enroll you when you purchase a ticket with a credit card. Others will sign you up over the phone, and you can begin getting credit for flights.

Once enrolled, indicate to the agent at check-in that you are a frequent flyer member. Also, when a frequent flyer sticker is required, make certain it is still on the ticket when it is collected. Neglect here could result in your not receiving mileage credit.

Airlines keep records of this mileage and usually notify you when you attain certain award levels. If you decide to claim the award, inform the airline. It will issue you an award certificate. Some airlines allow this certificate to be trans-ferred to a friend or sold to a coupon broker. Others permit the awards to be used only by family members.

COMPARING PROGRAMS

All major airlines except Braniff offer frequent flyer pro-grams. Eastern, Continental and New York Air participate in the One Pass plan. All programs accept two base awards on mileage flown: America West gives credit for the dollar amount of ticket purchases while Midway provides one cred-it for each one-way flight.

Frequent flyer programs, however, differ considerably in other respects.

Sign-Up Bonus: Many airlines offer mileage just for making an application. These bonuses range from 2,000 miles (American, United, USAir) to 5,000 miles (Pan Ameri-can). Special offers for limited time periods are also some-times available.

Minimum Mileage Credited: Most airlines credit a minimum number of miles regardless of the length of the flight. For example, a 150-mile flight on Northwest would receive 500 miles' credit. This minimum mileage ranges from 250 miles on Alaska to 750 miles on American and United.

Mileage to Earn Awards: The first award flyers in most programs qualify for is an upgrade from coach (or busi-ness class) to first class. When offered, these upgrades can be requested after earning between 5,000 points (Alaska) and 30,000 miles (Piedmont).

Most frequent flyers, however, do not take this award but continue accumulating mileage until they earn one or two free coach or first-class tickets. Many airlines, for example, offer two free coach tickets anywhere in the United States, including Hawaii, for 50,000 miles. PSA offers these tickets for only 20,000 miles while Delta requires 90,000 miles for two tickets to Hawaii.

Much greater mileage can qualify frequent flyers for trips outside the U.S., even around the world, and sometimes travel by train, ocean liner, or rental car, as well as other benefits, such as hotel accommodations or even ski-lift tickets.

Airline, Hotel, and Rental Car Tie-Ins: Many airlines allow mileage to be earned by using certain other airlines, hotels, or rental car companies. For example, Hawaiian and USAir have reciprocal agreements allowing mileage accumulated on one frequent flyer program to be used on the other.

Transferability of Awards: All airlines offering awards allow their use by any member of the frequent flyer's immediate family. Several, however, allow the transfer of awards to anyone else. The following table lists the features and benefits of the major frequent flyer programs.

FREQUENT FLYER PROGRAMS

Alaska
Gold Coast Travel Plan

Sign-up Bonus: None **Minimum Credit:** 250 mi. **Two Tickets to Hawaii:** 50,000 mi. **Airline Partners:** Hawaiian, Horizon, Mark Air, SAS, Thai **Hotel Partners:** Red Lion, West Mark **Car Rental Partners:** None **Transferability:** Yes

American
AAdvantage Program

Sign-up Bonus: 2,000 mi. **Minimum Credit:** 750 mi. **Two Tickets to Hawaii:** 50,000 mi. **Airline Partners:** British Air, KLM, Qantas, Singapore **Hotel Partners:** Inter-Continental, Sheraton, Wyndham **Car Rental Partners:** Avis **Transferability:** Yes

America West
FlightFUND

Sign-up Bonus: None **Minimum Credit:** None **Two Tickets to Hawaii:** NA **Airline Partners:** NA **Hotel Partners:** Compri, Doubletree, Marriott **Car Rental Partners:** Dollar **Transferability:** Yes

FREQUENT FLYER PROGRAMS

Continental
OnePass

Sign-up Bonus: 2,500 mi. **Minimum Credit:** 1,000 mi. **Two Tickets to Hawaii:** 50,000 mi. **Airline Partners:** Alitalia, Aer Lingus, Air France, British Caledonian, Sabena, SAS **Hotel Partners:** Compri, Doubletree, Marriott, Radisson, Regent Italian, Southern Pacific, Wyndham **Car Rental Partners:** General, Hertz, Thrifty **Transferability:** Yes

Delta
Frequent Flyer Program

Sign-up Bonus: 5,000 mi. **Minimum Credit:** 1,000 mi. **Two Tickets to Hawaii:** 90,000 mi. **Airline Partners:** Air Canada, Japan, Lufthansa, New Zealand, SwissAir **Hotel Partners:** Hyatt, Marriott, Preferred, Trusthouse **Car Rental Partners:** Alamo, Hertz, National **Transferability:** Yes[1/2]

Eastern
OnePass

Sign-up Bonus: 2,500 mi. **Minimum Credit:** 1,000 mi. **Two Tickets to Hawaii:** 50,000 mi. **Airline Partners:** Alitalia, Aer Lingus, Air France, British Caledonian, Sabena, SAS **Hotel Partners:** Compri, Doubletree, Marriott, Radisson, Regent Italian, Southern Pacific, Wyndham **Car Rental Partners:** General, Hertz, Thrifty **Transferability:** Yes

Hawaiian
Gold Plus Frequent Flyer Program

Sign-up Bonus: None **Minimum Credit:** 100 mi. **Two Tickets to Hawaii:** 12,000 mi. **Airline Partners:** Alaska, USAir **Hotel Partners:** Amfac **Car Rental Partners:** Avis, Dollar, Tropical **Transferability:** Yes

Midway
FlyersFirst

Sign-up Bonus: 4 points **Minimum Credit:** 1/2 point **Two Tickets to Hawaii:** NA **Airline Partners:** Iowa Air **Hotel Partners:** Omni **Car Rental Partners:** Budget, National **Transferability:** Yes

FREQUENT FLYER PROGRAMS

Northwest
WorldPerks

Sign-up Bonus: None **Minimun Credit:** 500 mi. **Two Tickets to Hawaii:** 80,000 mi. **Airline Partners:** NA **Hotel Partners:** Hyatt, Marriott, Radisson **Car Rental Partners:** National, Thrifty **Transferability:** Yes

PSA
Executive Flyer

Sign-up Bonus: 3,000 mi. **Minimun Credit:** 750 mi. **Two Tickets to Hawaii:** 60,000 mi. **Airline Partners:** Air Canada, Northwest, TWA, USAir **Hotel Partners:** Compri, Hilton, Marriott **Car Rental Partners:** Hertz **Transferability:** Yes

Pan Am
WorldPass

Sign-up Bonus: 5,000 mi. **Minimum Credit:** None **Two Tickets to Hawaii:** 40,000 mi. **Airline Partners:** NA **Hotel Partners:** NA **Car Rental Partners:** Hertz **Transferability:** Yes[1]

Piedmont
Frequent Flyer Bonus Program

Sign-up Bonus: 2,500 mi. **Minimum Credit:** 1,000 mi. **Two Tickets to Hawaii:** 80,000 mi. **Airline Partners:** British Air, TWA **Hotel Partners:** Marriott, Omni, Radisson, Stouffers **Car Rental Partners:** Europcar, Hertz, National, Tilden **Transferability:** Yes[2]

TWA
Frequent Flight Bonus Program

Sign-up Bonus: 3,000 mi. **Minimum Credit:** 750 mi. **Two Tickets to Hawaii:** NA **Airline Partners:** Eastern, Japan, PSA, Piedmont **Hotel Partners:** Hilton, Marriott **Car Rental Partners:** Hertz **Transferability:** Yes[2]

FREQUENT FLYER PROGRAMS

United
Mileage Plus

Sign-up Bonus: 2,000 mi. **Minimum Credit:** 750 mi. **Two Tickets to Hawaii:** 50,000 mi. **Airline Partners:** Air France, Air Wisconsin, Alitalia, Aspen, British Air, Cathay Pacific, Lufthansa, San Juan, SAS, SwissAir, West Air **Hotel Partners:** Hilton, Kempinski, Westin **Car Rental Partners:** Hertz **Transferability:** Yes[2]

USAir
Frequent Traveler Program

Sign-up Bonus: 2,000 mi. **Minimum Credit:** 500 mi. **Two Tickets to Hawaii:** NA **Airline Partners:** British Air, Finnair, Hawaiian, Lufthansa, PSA, Phillipine, UTA (France) **Hotel Partners:** Marriott, Omni **Car Rental Partners:** Budget, Hertz **Transferability:** Yes[2]

1. Must be accompanied by member
2. Only to family members

7

DELAYS AND CANCELLATIONS
How to Cope

Airline delays and cancellations are a growing problem. In the first 10 months of 1986, the Federal Aviation Administration (FAA) counted nearly 270,000 delays at the 22 airports it monitors. This total represented an increase of about 60,000 over the same period in 1985. And the FAA tally understates the problem because it counts only delays of 15 minutes or more. Thus, a flight with a 14-minute gate delay, a 14-minute taxi delay, a 14-minute airborne delay, and a 14-minute arrival delay would not be considered late even though it arrived nearly an hour behind schedule.

About a year ago, *USA Today* counted delayed arrivals at four major airports – Atlanta, Denver, Los Angeles, and Washington National. Thirty percent of the 1,955 flights arrived more than 15 minutes after their scheduled arrival times. More disturbing, even in good weather 55 Delta flights and 40 Eastern flights in and out of Atlanta were late at least 70 percent of the time, according to the U.S. Department of Transportation.

As a result, complaints about delays and cancellations are at an all time high. In the first six months of 1987, 40 percent (5,570) of the complaints filed with the U.S. DOT concerned these flight problems. That number was up from 3,299 for all of 1986 and 2,718 for all of 1985.

Not only are delays and cancellations problems in themselves, but they generate other problems. These include sitting for long periods in a stationary plane that may have its air conditioning turned off, connections that may be missed, baggage more likely to be misrouted, friends kept waiting at the airport, and appointments that may be missed.

The reasons for delays are myriad. Many relate to deregulation. More discount fares increased the number of airline passengers. They also cut the profits of airlines, encouraging them to move to a "more efficient" hub and spoke system where dozens of flights arrive and depart in short periods of time. Some airlines even schedule more flights than could physically arrive at and depart from an airport in a given time period. The federal government contributed to the problem by reducing the number of air controllers and by failing to allocate sufficient trust funds for airport expansion. To date, it has also refused to require airlines to spread out flights and to publish more realistic timetables.

AVOIDING AND COPING WITH DELAYS

Here are some strategies for avoiding and coping with delays.

Flight Selection: Try to book flights that are least likely to be delayed. You can greatly minimize the chances of delay by flying off-peak or on weekends before Sunday afternoon, by avoiding busy hub airports, and by avoiding airlines whose planes are often late.

Generally speaking, peak periods are rush hours — early morning, late afternoon, and early evening. The *USA Today* survey of delays at four airports found that the highest percentage of delayed arrivals occurred in the latter two periods, the lowest percentage in the morning and early afternoon. The table below indicates the best and worst times to land at these airports, with delay rates.

BEST AND WORST ARRIVAL TIMES
(with Delay Rates)

Airline	Best	Worst
Washington National	2-3 p.m. (5%)	6-7 p.m. (93%)
Los Angeles Int'l	8-9 a.m. (20%)	3-4 p.m. (67%)
Denver	8-9 p.m. (4%)	5-6 p.m. (over 50%)
Atlanta	1-2 p.m. (2%)	7-8 p.m. (41%)

A second flight selection strategy is to avoid hub airports. This is impossible if you must depart from or arrive at one of these hubs. But you can often avoid stopping at a busy hub en route. If traveling coast to coast and forced to make a stop, frequent flyers often go to great lengths to avoid Chicago, selecting Kansas City or even St. Louis, regardless of the airline implications. Listed below are the major hubs — if possible, avoid them.

HUB AIRPORTS	AIRLINES
Atlanta	Delta, Eastern
Baltimore	Piedmont
Boston	Northwest
Charlotte	Piedmont
Chicago	United, American
Cincinnati	Delta
Dallas/Ft. Worth	American, Delta
Dayton	Piedmont
Denver	United, Continental
Detroit	Northwest
Houston	Continental
Kansas City (MO)	Eastern, Braniff
Los Angeles	Delta
Memphis	Northwest
Miami	Eastern, Pan American
Minneapolis/St. Paul	Northwest
Nashville	American

HUB AIRPORTS	AIRLINES
New York (JFK)	Pan American, TWA
Orlando	Piedmont
Philadelphia	USAir
Phoenix	America West, Southwest
Pittsburgh	USAir
Raleigh, Durham	American
Salt Lake City	Delta
San Francisco	United
St. Louis	TWA
Seattle	United, Alaska
Syracuse	Piedmont
Washington (Dulles)	United, Pan American

Source: *USA Today*

A third strategy for avoiding delays is to choose airlines with the best on-time records. Here are three sets of on-time statistics recently published by *The Wall Street Journal,* for July and August 1986, *USA Today,* for January through May, 1987 and the U.S. Department of Transportation, for September, 1987. Because these statistics were supplied by the airlines they may be biased. Moreover, these percentages certainly vary depending on the type of routes flown. For instance, airlines concentrating flights in the congested northeastern corridor are more likely to have low ratings. However, they do point out that the on-time records vary between airlines and reinforce the notion of avoiding hub airports. In late 1987 information on the on-time perform-ance of individual flights will be available from travel agents and at ticket counters.

ON-TIME PERCENTAGES

Airline	Jul-Aug 1986	Jan-May 1987	September 1987
American	64%	63%	86%
Continental	75%	60%	81%
Delta	63%	N/A	72%
Eastern	60%	61%	80%
Northwest	N/A	54%	69%
Pan American	65%	71%	74%
Piedmont	N/A	75%	80%
Southwest	83%	N/A	82%
TWA	N/A	58%	78%
United	61%	67%	79%
USAir	N/A	66%	67%

Airport Strategies: Airlines may report cancellations over the phone, but rarely delays (except for some caused by weather within four hours of the scheduled departure). So you must go to the airport and take your chances. Once there, inquire about the status of your flight—first at the check-in counter, if you're checking in baggage, then at the gate. If you are purchasing your ticket at the airport, before doing so, inquire whether there is a delay. If it is lengthy, investigate other flights. Since airlines are not always forthcoming with information on delays, this may require some persistence.

If, on the other hand, you purchased your ticket before getting to the airport and discover a lengthy delay, most other airlines will accept your ticket. If they refuse, ask the first airline to book you on the second airline and pay any fare difference. Since they are not required to do so, you will have to make a pretty forceful argument.

If you cannot transfer to another flight, sometimes the airline will provide a meal. If you are diverted to another airport with a lengthy delay, airlines including American and Eastern will supply lodging and a meal. Keep in mind, however, that to get any compensation you nearly always must ask. Because the airline is not required to give you anything, your persuasive powers may be the determining factor in receiving compensation for delays.

On the Plane: If you are trapped on a plane that is sitting on the runway, the only way to get off is to become violently ill or to create such a ruckus that you are taken into custody. One way to tolerate these delays is to write complaint letters to the airline president, to the DOT, and to your senator and congressman. In addition to being a cathartic exercise, your efforts will help bring about changes.

AVOIDING AND COPING WITH CANCELLATIONS

Cancellations are more difficult to predict, and therefore avoid, than delays. Frequent flyers are convinced that many airlines simply cancel some flights because there are few passengers. They are most likely to do this when there is another flight to the same destination, leaving around the same time, with empty seats. While the published DOT flight problem complaint statistics do not separate delays from cancellations, we do know many flyers have complained about cancellations by Continental.

To learn about cancellations at the earliest possible moment, call the airline before leaving for the airport. If your flight is cancelled, consider asking the airline to book you on another flight at no additional charge. While not required to, they will usually do so, but usually on one of their own planes. You may wish to call other airlines yourself to book another flight, making certain to ask them if they will accept your original ticket. If you are at the airport, you can often lobby more effectively for transfer to another airline in person than over the phone.

If stranded at the airport overnight because of a cancellation, insist that you be given lodging and meals. Again, though not required to, airlines sometimes supply these amenities – but you must ask. If your request is turned down, don't give up. Airline representatives often have a great deal of discretionary power in these matters, so try someone else. If this doesn't work, ask to see the manager in charge.

RATING THE AIRLINES

Given the limitations of the on-time statistics, the most reliable index of airline performance on delays and cancellations is the DOT complaint data on flight problems. According to these figures, Delta is the only large airline with a good rating. Continental has by far the worst, but Eastern and Northwest also have very poor ratings. United also has a poor rating, even worse than that of Pan American, which has a poorer reputation among travelers.

The following table allows you to compare the delay and cancellation records of the major airlines, based on consumer complaints registered with the DOT from January 1986 through June 1987.

CONSUMER COMPLAINTS
Delays and Cancellations

Airline	Complaints per 100,000 Passengers	Evaluation
Alaska	0.19	Good
AmericaWest	0.38	Good
American	0.62	Fair
Braniff	0.63	Fair
Continental	4.60	Very Poor
Delta	0.34	Good
Eastern	2.22	Very Poor
Hawaiian	0.91	Fair
Midway	0.81	Fair
Northwest	2.98	Very Poor
PSA	0.32	Good
Pan American	1.25	Poor
Piedmont	0.55	Fair
Southwest	0.22	Good
TWA	1.85	Poor
United	1.36	Poor
USAir	0.65	Fair

Higher index numbers mean poorer performance

8

SEATING
How to Maximize Comfort

For most of us, cost and convenience are the primary factors in selecting a flight. Once on the plane, you may wish you had paid more attention to seat selection. Sitting too close to the smoking section, being wedged into a narrow middle seat, or being tucked behind a bulkhead when you wanted to see the film are all reasons why you may wish to consider seat selection before your next flight.

There are three basic strategies for maximizing seating comfort. First, try to get into first class or business class without having to purchase an expensive ticket. Second, select an airline likely to have roomy seating and a less-than-full load. Third, reserve in advance a seat that maximizes comfort values, such as legroom, access to the aisles, or distance from the smoking section.

GETTING INTO FIRST CLASS OR BUSINESS CLASS

Sitting in first class is the easiest way to maximize comfort. Compared to coach, first-class seats are large and well-spaced with plenty of elbow-room. There are fewer passengers for each flight attendant and for each lavatory, and you are usually first off the plane.

The problem is that an overwhelming majority of travelers do not believe the amenities of first class are worth the additional cost, typically 20 to 50 percent above full coach fare and much higher than discounted coach fares. There are, however, a couple of ways to fly first class on a coach fare. The easiest and most common is to use mileage accumulated on a frequent flyer program for an upgrade. See the previous chapter on *Frequent Flyer Programs*. The only cost here is that this mileage will not be available for such other bonuses as a free ticket.

The other way is to try to take advantage of a full or over-sold flight. This can be done by being one of the last to board on a full flight in the hope that your assigned seat will be occupied by someone else. To expedite departure, the flight attendant will often move you to first class. Using this ploy, there is little risk here of being forced off the plane. Even if all seats are taken, airlines offer incentives nearly always sufficient to persuade enough passengers to give up their seats. The real risk is of being forced to accept an inferior coach seat (for example, middle rather than aisle) when the coach section is not full.

Another strategy when a flight is oversold is to ask gate personnel for an upgrade if they are planning to seat coach passengers in first class. Sometimes these gatekeepers are willing to assign your seat to another passenger, then move you to a vacant first-class seat.

Business Class: A less expensive alternative to first class is business class, which may cost only a modest amount more that full coach fare. In this class, seats are roomier, there is usually more space for carry on luggage, and as the table below indicates, travelers receive many of the amenities enjoyed by first class passengers.

BUSINESS CLASS FEATURES OFFERED BY THE MAJOR AIRLINES*

Features	Percent Offering
Separate check in	100%
Free drinks	100%
Permanent separate cabin	98%
Choice of meal entrees	96%
Advance seating selection	87%
Priority luggage handling	87%
Wide seats	83%
Gift or toiletry kit	80%
Electronic headsets	78%
Private airport lounges	78%
Separate or late boarding	78%
Extra carry-on space	74%
Separate lavatory	67%
Extra baggage allowance	63%

* Based on a survey of 46 U.S. and foreign airlines

SELECTING THE LEAST CROWDED FLIGHT

If you are not able to fly first or business class inexpensively, consider selecting among flights, comparable in other ways, by assessing crowding inside the cabin. The important factors are how full the plane is and how the seats are configured.

The Load Factor: The load factor is an airline term describing the percentage of seats that are filled. Planes that are two-thirds filled are invariably more comfortable to ride in than those that are full. You can use empty middle seats for books, glasses, empty trays, and elbows. Also, cabin service is quicker, and lines to use the lavatories are shorter.

How do you find flights that are less than full? As a general rule, off-peak flights tend to be less full than peak ones. Also, airlines, such as Pan American and Braniff with tarnished reputations tend to have less full cabins than more popular airlines, like American and United. This is supported by 1986 data on load factors for major airlines. Therefore, when choosing between popular and unpopular airlines, select the latter.There is, however, a more reliable method available to those who purchase their tickets shortly before the departure day — a call to the airline to learn how full the flight is. If there are no extra seats, it may still be possible to switch to a less than full flight.

DOMESTIC LOAD FACTORS (1986)

Airline	Load Factor (Percent Full)
American	65.6%
Continental	62.7%
Delta	57.4%
Eastern	60.6%
Northwest	54.9%
Pan American	51.4%
Piedmont	58.7%
TWA	59.5%
United	65.6%
USAir	61.1%

Source: U.S. Department of Transportation

The Seat Factor: The second factor affecting cabin crowding is the size and configuration of the seats. The important size factors are the seat widths and the distance between rows (or pitch). Coach seats range from 18-1/2 to 22 inches in width. The distance between rows ranges from 30 to 37 inches, with most between 31 and 33 inches. The most important aspect of seating configuration is the number of middle seats. The fewer middle seats, the more elbowroom in a cabin.

Unfortunately, there is no simple guideline that will enable you to identify flights with the most spacious seating. The same plane, used by two different airlines, will often have different seating plans. In addition, each airline uses a number of different planes.

Consumer Reports Travel Letter has analyzed the seating used by different airlines in terms of aircraft, distance between rows (seat pitch), seat width, and seats per row. They combined this information into a "comfort index" that summarizes seating spaciousness. Below is the information and the index. The higher the index number, the greater the comfort.

Now in its third year of publication, *CRTL* accepts no advertising, free trips, or gifts. *CRTL* is a monthly newsletter on travel for consumers. Subscriptions are $37 for one year, $57 for two years. Single copies are available for $5. For more information, call 800-525-0643; in Colorado, 303-447-9330.

SEATING COMFORT

Airline	Aircraft	Seating Plan	Comfort Index	Comfort Rating
Alaska	727	3-3	74	Fair
	MD80	2-3	77	Good
	737	3-3	71	Fair
America West	757	3-3	69	Poor
	737	3-3	69	Poor
American	747	3-4-3	74	Fair
	DC10	2-5-2	75	Good
	767	2-3-2	78	Good
	727	3-3	66	Poor
	DC9	2-3	77	Good
	737-300	3-3	74	Fair
	737-200	3-3	81	Very Good
	BAE146	2-3	85	Very Good
Braniff	727	3-3	77	Good

SEATING COMFORT

Airline	Aircraft	Seating Plan	Comfort Index	Comfort Rating
Continental	747	3-4-3	74	Fair
	DC10	2-5-2	78	Good
	A300	2-4-2	75	Good
	727	3-3	69	Poor
	MD80	2-3	77	Good
	737	3-3	69	Poor
	DC9	2-3	77	Good
Delta	DC10	2-5-2	75	Good
	L1011	2-5-2	75	Good
	767	2-3-2	78	Good
	DC8	3-3	69	Poor
	757	3-3	69	Poor
	727	3-3	69	Poor
	MD80	2-3	77	Good
	737-300	3-3	66	Poor
	737-200	3-3	69	Poor
	DC9	2-3	75	Good
Eastern	DC10	2-5-2	73	Fair
	L1011	2-5-2	75	Good
	A300	2-4-2	73	Fair
	757	3-3	69	Poor
	727-200	3-3	69	Poor
	727-100	3-3	74	Fair
	DC9	2-3	72	Fair
Hawaiian	L1011	3-4-3	67	Poor
	DC8-63	3-3	74	Fair
	DC8-62	3-3	64	Very Poor
	DC9	2-3	72	Fair
Midway	737	3-3	64	Very Poor
	DC9-30	2-3	65	Poor
	DC9-10	2-3	67	Poor

SEATING COMFORT

Airline	Aircraft	Seating Plan	Comfort Index	Comfort Rating
Northwest	747	3-4-3	69	Poor
	DC10	2-5-2	74	Fair
	757	3-3	69	Poor
	727	3-3	69	Poor
	MD80	2-3	77	Good
	DC9	2-3	77	Good
PSA	MD80	2-3	77	Good
	BAE146	2-3	85	Very Good
Pan American	747	3-4-3	74	Fair
	A300	2-4-2	78	Good
	A310	2-4-2	70	Fair
	727	3-3	69	Poor
	737	3-3	71	Fair
Piedmont	767	2-3-2	78	Good
	727	3-3	69	Poor
	737	3-3	69	Poor
	F28	2-3	67	Poor
Southwest	737-300	3-3	69	Poor
	737-200	3-3	66	Poor
TWA	747	3-4-3	77	Good
	L1011	2-5-2	83	Very Good
	767	2-3-2	78	Good
	727	3-3	69	Poor
	MD80	2-3	77	Good
	DC9	2-3	77	Good
United	747	3-4-3	74	Fair
	747SP	3-4-3	72	Fair
	DC10-30	2-5-2	75	Good
	DC10-10	2-5-2	78	Good
	L1011	3-4-3	73	Fair
	767	2-3-2	83	Very Good
	727-200	3-3	69	Poor
	727-100	3-3	74	Fair
	737	3-3	69	Poor

SEATING COMFORT				
Airline	Aircraft	Seating Plan	Comfort Index	Comfort Rating
USAir	727	3-3	69	Poor
	737	3-3	69	Poor
	DC9	2-3	78	Good
	BAC111	2-3	72	Fair

SELECTING A CONVENIENT SEAT

Here are some other factors to consider when selecting a seat.

Access to Aisle: Obviously, on full flights it is easier to get into the aisle if you are sitting in an aisle seat. The downside of an aisle seat is that you have to get up, or at least move in your seat, to allow window and middle seat passengers access to the aisle. This can be especially inconvenient if you wish to sleep or work.

Quick Departure: On planes with front cabin doors, the further forward you sit, the more quickly you can get off the plane. Since each row usually gets off before the next, the only advantage of an aisle seat is that it is easier to remove luggage from overhead compartments without being rushed.

View: For a good view outside the plane, the obvious choice is a window seat. However, make sure that your seat is not over the wing.

Movies: Longer flights often have an inflight film. The seats in the center cluster of wide-body jets allow less interrupted viewing than those on the aisles. In the latter, your vision is blocked anytime someone walks down the aisle.

Also, to get a clear picture, you should not sit in the first or second row or toward the back. The latter is especially important if the film is shown on a television monitor.

Avoiding Smoke: Since cabin air is recirculated to an extent, you can never avoid cigarette smoke completely. Still, sitting away from smoking sections in coach and first class will minimize discomfort.

Children: If you have children, the first row of seats behind the bulkhead offers extra leg room and space for them to play without disturbing others. Rows with exit windows are often wider than other rows, but parents with very young children are prohibited from these rows. Tip: if two of you are flying with a lap child, request the window and aisle seat. If the plane is not full, you are likely to retain the middle seat for yourself because few people volunteer to sit in middle seats. If you are paying for a child, and want to bring a car seat to offer the child extra safety protection, remember it must have an FAA approval sticker to be allowed on the plane.

Avoiding Children: If sitting near children bothers you, when checking in ask for a seat away from any children that may be on board.

Legroom: The seats in the first row behind the bulkhead generally have a little more legroom. This is also true of seats on aisles and next to window exits.

Carry On Luggage: Middle seats have the most room for luggage under the seat in the row ahead. Aisle seats provide easy access to overhead baggage compartments if you need something during the flight.

Reclining Seats: Seats just ahead of bulkheads and in emergency exit rows may not fully recline.

A Smooth Ride: Seats over the wing give the most stable ride – seats at the rear of the plane, the least.

The two factors that some travelers often believe are influenced by seating but are not are safety and speed of cabin service. In fact, no area of seating is consistently safer than others. In some crashes, those sitting in the rear have been most likely to survive while in other accidents passengers toward the front have been safest.

The best way to get the seat you prefer is to reserve one as early as possible. Nearly all major airlines now offer advance seat assignments when you (or the travel agent) purchase the tickets. You can also get your boarding passes with your ticket. This may be of limited value because these passes can be quickly obtained at the gate and because they increase the chance that someone else will be assigned to your seat. How soon in advance of a flight you can get a seat assignment varies from airline to airline. The table below indicates which airlines offer advance seat selection and how soon it is available.

ADVANCE SEAT SELECTION

Airline	Available?	How Far in Advance?
Alaska	Yes	28 days
American	Yes	1 year
Braniff	Yes	330 days
Continental	Yes	18 days
Delta	Yes	31 days
Eastern	Yes	29 days
Hawaiian	Yes	30 days
Midway	Yes	4-6 weeks
Northwest	Yes	2 months
PSA	No[1]	
Pan American	Yes	331 days
Piedmont	Yes	29 days
Southwest	No	
TWA	Yes	30 days
United	Yes	331 days
USAir	Yes	21 days

1. Unless a member of frequent flyer program.

A new limitation on advance seat selection has recently been introduced by several major airlines on those purchasing heavily discounted fares. Under this policy, passengers buying max savers — those with the largest discounts — are not permitted to select seats until the day of the flight. This represents a response to complaints by full-fare travelers that they cannot reserve desired seats because these have already been taken by passengers purchasing discounted tickets well in advance of the flight.

If you are not satisfied with the seat you selected in advance, you may have an opportunity to change it at check in. If seat selection is not computerized, you can look at the seating chart to see which seats are taken and which are available. Just before the gate closes, you can move your seat to a window or aisle with a free middle seat. This is more difficult to do if a computer is being used since you are more dependent on the gate staff. You can, however, request a seat next to an unfilled middle, but you may end up with other undesirable seating features, such as proximity to smokers.

COPING WITH OPEN SEATING

Most airlines have nearly eliminated open seating, where you simply board the plane and find a seat. The exceptions are shuttle services, small planes, and on planes served by a malfunctioning computer. Without seat assignments, your only recourse is to board early.

9

BAGGAGE AND PETS
Ensuring Their Arrival and Safety

It is no surprise that most air travelers have experienced or heard of a lost baggage horror story. *Frequent Flyer Magazine* estimated that in 1983 two million bags were either lost or damaged. In the first six months of 1987, the U.S. Department of Transportation received 2,817 complaints related to baggage.

Most flyers who check luggage receive it at their destination in good condition. However, in the event that baggage is damaged, delayed, or lost, the costs can be considerable. The worst is the loss of expensive items for which airlines are not required to provide compensation. Less damaging financially, but greatly inconvenient, is the temporary or permanent loss of clothing or equipment used for business or vacation. When luggage is lost, the frequent delays and frustrations suffered trying to obtain compensation are added aggravations. This chapter explains how to prevent, or minimize, the chances that baggage will be delayed or lost, and when it is, how to obtain adequate reimbursement.

CARRYING ON LUGGAGE

We strongly recommend packing lightly and carrying your

baggage on the plane whenever possible. In addition to insuring that you and your luggage arrive together, this will also save you any delay, and anxiety, at the baggage carousel.

Most airlines place few restrictions on carry-on baggage that they enforce. Yet, they do require that items be able to fit in the overhead compartments, under seats, or in hangup closets. Most large suitcases will not fit in these locations. Also, because more travelers are carrying on their luggage, it is becoming difficult to find storage space on board.

Here are some tips for carrying on luggage. First, travel only with the bare essentials. Avoid taking heavy items such as extra shoes, books, and mechanical and electrical equipment. Second, make sure your bag can be stored in an overhead compartment or fits under a seat. Third, if the flight is full, and many passengers are carrying on luggage, stand in line at the gate to be one of the first persons seated in your section. This will ensure that you have available space in an overhead compartment. On these flights, however, make sure other passengers do not place heavy baggage on top of your clothes bag or loose clothing.

CHECKING LUGGAGE

If you are unable to carry on luggage, here are some tips to minimize delays and avoid loss.

Flight Selection: Luggage is most likely to be misplaced on flights where you transfer airlines and least likely to be lost on direct or nonstop flights where you stay on the same plane. Thus, if you have a choice, select the latter. And if you must transfer planes, try to stay on the same airline. Baggage handlers sometimes will make a greater effort to move luggage quickly between their own planes than to that of a competitor. Moreover, their task is easier because the planes of one airline tend to dock at the same pier.

If you must transfer airlines, and have plenty of time, consider claiming your luggage from the first airline and checking it in at the second. This option, however, is only feasible at airports where one walks near the baggage area to get to the second plane. For example, the prospect of traveling from a pier at Atlanta back to the baggage area in the main terminal, then out to another pier may have little appeal to you, even if this trip safeguards your luggage. And you may miss your connecting flight.

Packing: Pack as if you will never see the checked luggage again, and also as if this baggage will be dropped from the top of a four-story building. With an increase in tight connections at hub airports, baggage handlers are more interested in speed than in gentle treatment.

Certain items should never be checked. These include the things you will need as soon as you land – toiletries, prescription drugs, and glasses.

In addition, you should not check passports, travelers' checks, airline tickets, jewelry, negotiable stocks or securities, cash, irreplaceable business documents, and items with sentimental value. If you must bring these along on your trip, carry them on the plane. Finally, do not pack sensitive equipment, glass, china, and liquids in breakable containers.

If you must check luggage containing items of great financial value, purchase "excess valuation" from the airline. This protection costs between $.50 and $2 for each $100 of coverage. It is important because airlines are liable for a maximum of only $1,250 in losses per ticketed passenger. Also, airlines may give insured bags special attention.

There are also items that you are legally prohibited from bringing on the plane, whether carried on or checked in. These are aerosols, such as polishes, waxes, and cleaners; corrosives, such as acids, cleaners, and wet cell batteries; flammables, such as paints, thinners, lighter fluids, cleaners, and adhesives; explosives, such as fireworks, flares, and loaded firearms; radioactives, such as betascopes and uninstalled pacemakers; and compressed gases, such as tear gas, oxygen cylinders and full diver's tanks. Loose book matches or safety matches may be carried only on your person.

Baggage Limits: As you pack, also consider limits airlines have placed on the size, number, and weight of bags they will carry free of additional charges. The table below indicates these limits. Note that most airlines permit up to three pieces per passenger with a weight limit of 70 pounds. The cost of an additional piece ranges, among airlines, from $5 to $25 and up.

BAGGAGE LIMITS WITHOUT CHARGE

Airline	Max. No. of Items	Maximum Weight lbs.	Charge for Add'l Item
Alaska	3	70	$30 and up
America West	3	40	$10
American	3	70	$30 and up
Braniff	3	70	$10 and up
Continental	3	70	$30 and up
Delta	3	70	$30 and up
Eastern	3	70	$25 and up
Hawaiian	2	66	$25 and up
Midway	3	70	$15
Northwest	3	70	$30 and up
Pan American	3	70	$25 and up
Piedmont	3	70	$20
Southwest	3	60	$5
TWA	3	70	$30 and up
United	3	70	$25 and up
USAir	3	70	$20

Check In: Careful check in procedure can also minimize baggage delays and losses. Check in at least 30 minutes before departure. This will give the airline adequate time to transport your bags from the ticket counter to the plane. Never check in luggage less than 15 minutes before departure. This is the surest way to increase the chances of your bags being sent on another plane. In fact, within 15 minutes of departure, most airlines will not guarantee that your luggage will travel on your plane. Eastern's policy has been that, if items go on the next flight, you have to pay for delivery. United's has been that it will not even check in items. Within

10 minutes of departure, Continental requires you to sign a disclaimer saying that the airline is not responsible for lost baggage.

When you check in, make sure a name, address, and phone number is on the outside (and inside) of your bags. It is wise to use business rather than home phone and address since the latter may alert potential burglars that you are not at home. Some people mark their luggage with fluorescent or brightly colored tape so that it is easily recognizable. Make certain that each checked item is tagged, that tags from previous flights are removed, that the information on the tag — destination airport and flight number — is correct, and that you have claim checks for each. *Do not throw away claim checks until you have unpacked your bags and checked for damage or pilferage of contents.*

Tip: Some travelers, especially around Christmas holidays, send certain items ahead by post. This avoids struggling with them at the airport and the risk of losing them after check in.

BAGGAGE COMPLAINTS

Baggage problems are the second leading cause of air travel complaints. Here are the typical problems which lead this complaint list:

Damage: Passengers complain about damaged items for which airlines refuse to provide compensation, such as fragile or perishable goods, those that the airline decides were packed inadequately, and damaged items inside a bag on which there is no evidence of external damage.

Delays: Travelers also complain when baggage is sent on another flight, forcing them to wait at the airport or go without this luggage for a period of time. The problems increase when passengers move on to another city and the airline refuses to send on found items without charge.

Losses: Passengers are most upset when their baggage

is lost. It sometimes takes months for the airline finally to declare an item lost and to begin processing claims for reimbursement.

Travelers complain more frequently about some airlines than about others. The following table lists the DOT baggage complaint ratios and overall rating of major airlines in 1986 and the first six months of 1987. Note that there is a huge range of ratios. Those airlines with *very poor* ratings — Continental, Pan American, and Hawaiian — had at least ten times the number of baggage complaints as those with *very good* ratings — Southwest and Delta.

RATING AIRLINES ON BAGGAGE HANDLING		
Airline	Complaints per 100,000 Passengers	Evaluation
Alaska	0.28	Good
America West	0.33	Good
American	0.37	Good
Braniff	0.68	Fair
Continental	2.87	Very Poor
Delta	0.13	Very Good
Eastern	0.87	Poor
Hawaiian	1.40	Very Poor
Midway	0.30	Good
Northwest	0.87	Poor
PSA	0.30	Good
Pan American	1.69	Very Poor
Piedmont	0.19	Good
Southwest	0.12	Very Good
TWA	1.03	Poor
United	0.67	Fair
USAir	0.21	Good

COPING WITH BAGGAGE DELAYS AND LOSSES

If a checked bag fails to arrive on your flight, or arrives in a damaged condition, report this at once to the airline. If you transferred airlines, this is the last one on which you rode. If it arrives open or unlocked, check immediately for damaged or lost contents.

Delayed Bags: If the baggage is missing, assume that it will be found. With the aid of an extensive computer system used by most airlines, well over 90 percent of missing bags are eventually tracked down and returned. Before leaving the airport, however, fill out a form describing the bag, listing its contents, and providing other information, even if the airline says it will be on the next flight. Keep a copy of this form for your records. Before leaving the airport, ask the airline to agree to deliver the bag free of charge and keep a record of the name of the employee who agrees to do this.

Most airlines cover reasonable expenses related to these delays. They authorize airport personnel to offer money for the purchase of toiletries or even some clothing. If sports equipment is missing, they may pay for the rental of replacements. For replacement clothing, they might offer to absorb only half its purchase cost. If you insist on paying nothing, they may agree to cover the full cost but require the return of the new clothing to the airline.

Damages: If your suitcase arrives smashed or torn, most airlines will pay for repairs and compensate you for damages to contents. Their maximum liability, however, is $1,250 per passenger. This applies only to flights on large aircraft (over 60 seats) and on smaller planes when they are on a ticket with a large one.

Even though you report the damages immediately, later you will be asked to provide supporting evidence for damage claims. This is easiest to do if you paid for items within the past several years by check or credit card and kept your payment records. Do not, however, expect payment for at least a month and possibly for several months.

Lost Luggage: If you do not receive a delayed bag within three days, it is unlikely that it will ever be returned. Sometime after this, usually a month or longer, the airline will declare the bag officially lost. At this point, the airline may well request additional information about the items lost, including proof of purchase. Then they will depreciate the value of most items before computing the total amount of compensation. TWA, for example, depreciates a suitcase fully over seven years, yet will reimburse clothes purchased within six months at full cost. The maximum liability per passenger is $1,250 unless you purchased excess coverage. As with damaged goods, be pleased if compensation arrives in several weeks. It may take as long as four months.

Means of Redress: If you are dissatisfied with the way the airline handles your claim for damages or losses, you have other means of redress. In addition to notifying the U.S. Department of Transportation, you should consider filing a complaint with state or local protection agencies which have jurisdiction in the area where the airport is located. As a last resort, file a grievance with a local small claims court. To receive a satisfactory settlement when pursuing these options, however, make certain that you can document losses beyond any compensation the airline is willing to provide and that your claim is below the $1,250 maximum.

TRAVELING WITH PETS

If an animal is small enough, most airlines allow you to travel with it in the cabin. But it must fit into a kennel no larger than 17 by 12 by 7-1/2 inches. Pets that do not fit into this container must travel by kennel in the baggage hold, where they may experience discomfort from air pressure changes. If you are changing planes, plan to reclaim this kennel and recheck it for the next flight.

On many airlines, there is a pet surcharge of $25 to $30 for each kennel, carried or shipped, for a flight of any length. Some airlines sell kennels to customers.

If you plan to travel with an animal, the most important thing to do is to inform the airline well in advance. Some airlines restrict the number of pets to one per coach and one per first class. If you must travel with a pet on the spur of the moment, remember that airlines require at least 24 hours notice.

10

FOOD AND OTHER CABIN SERVICES

What Are the Options?

Even though most air travelers rate seating comfort above food and other cabin services, about eight percent of complaints received by the U.S. Department of Transportation relate to customer service, which includes meals and cabin services. An even larger number of passengers complain to the airlines themselves. In 1984, for example, nearly 4,000 United passengers filed grievances about food with the airline. This chapter explains meal options and other cabin services, including the new air phones.

MEALS AND THEIR AVAILABILITY

In order to economize, most airlines have been trying to cut back on meal expenses. This cost-cutting can take the form of substituting cold snacks for warm meals, or making little effort to improve the standard dinner with its glutinous sauce, watery vegetable, wilted lettuce, dry cake, chemical salad dressing, and nondairy creamer. The good news is that airlines have diversified their menus somewhat, making available fish or pasta as well as beef or chicken, and despite passenger complaints, even serving soup and sandwiches for lunch.

The length of the trip is the most important factor in determining what kind of meals you can expect on a flight. The longer it is, the more food you will be served. The table below indicates what meals you are likely to receive. Keep in mind, however, that airlines may change their policies. When you make reservations, inquire about meal service – and request special meals at that time.

FOOD AND BEVERAGE SERVICE What's Likely to be Served				
Length of Flight	Beverages	Breakfast	Cold Meal	Hot Meal
1 hour	●			
2 hours	●	● (or)	●	
3 hours	●	● (or)		●
4 hours	●	● (or)		●
5-7 hours	●	● (or)	● (and)	●

Many travelers are unaware that airlines offer a variety of special meals – low sodium, vegetarian, diabetic, low calorie, to mention only a few. To be served one of these meals, you must place an order in advance, typically at least two days before the flight. It is probably most convenient for you or your travel agent to do this when purchasing the ticket. The DOT, however, has received a number of complaints that specially-ordered meals were not provided. One traveler, for example, claimed he was not served a requested diabetic meal on five consecutive flights. The table below lists the availability of 12 types of meals offered by the major airlines.

SPECIAL MEALS

Airline	CH	KO	LS	VE	VP	DI	LCH	LCA	HY	GF	OR	SF
Alaska	•	•	•	•	•	•	•	•	•		•	•
America West												
American[1]	•	•	•		•	•	•	•	•			•
Braniff		•										
Continental[2]		•	•	•	•							
Delta	•	•	•	•	•	•	•	•	•			•
Eastern	•	•	•	•			•		•			•
Hawaiian	•	•	•	•	•	•	•	•				•
Midway		•	•	•	•							
Northwest	•	•	•	•	•	•	•			•		•
PSA												
Pan American	•	•	•	•	•	•	•		•			•
Piedmont	•	•	•	•			•		•			•
Southwest												
TWA	•	•	•			•	•	•				•
United	•	•	•		•	•	•	•				
USAir	•	•	•	•	•	•	•	•	•	•		

KEY: CH = Children's; **KO** = Kosher; **LS** = Low Sodium; **VE** = Vegetarian (eggs); **VP** = Vegetarian (pure); **DI** = Diabetic; **LCH** = Low Cholesterol; **LCA** = Low Calorie; **HY** = Hypoglycemic; **GF** = Gluten Free; **OR** = Oriental; **SF** = Seafood

OTHER CABIN SERVICES

Because airlines have recently increased load factors and sometimes reduced the number of flight attendants on flights, cabin service is not as attentive as it once was. Try to keep in mind, though, that this is rarely the fault of the attendants themselves. On short flights with a full load, they hardly have time to serve and clean up beverages and food, let alone respond to individual requests. To increase the chances of good service, try to select flights that are not full.

Specific cabin services beyond meals vary depending on the airline and the length of flight. Some airlines like Midway routinely provide hot towels to all passengers near the end of the trip. Almost all planes carry magazines, and a few offer free newspapers and coffee at the gate. These extra services are more frequently provided at busy, competitive airports served by several airlines. On long flights, airlines including United, American, USAir, and TWA will rent headsets that allow listening to audio programs or to a movie's sound track. Prices range from $2 at TWA to $4 at United and American.

Airfone: A new service available on many planes allows passengers to place telephone calls while in flight. Airlines with phones on at least some of their planes include American, Continental, Eastern, Delta, Jet America, Midway, Northwest, Piedmont, Pan American, TWA, and United. Widebody planes usually have four phones, and smaller planes have two. To place a call, you insert a credit card into a slot on the wall unit. After the card is verified, you can remove the cordless phone and bring it to your seat. Individual calls are limited to 45 minutes. When they are completed, you return the handset to the wall unit and recover your credit card. The charge is $7.50 for the first three minutes and $1.25 for each additional minute anywhere in the U.S. and Canada.

11

PASSENGER SAFETY
What Are the Risks and How Can They Be Minimized?

Despite all the news coverage and commentary on the deterioration of airline safety, flying remains one of the safest means of travel. Statistically, you are 100 times more likely to die in a car crash than in an airline accident. Furthermore, as the following table indicates, the number of fatal accidents and fatalities has not risen appreciably.

Year	Fatal Accidents	Fatalities	Fatal Accidents per 1 Million Flights
1977	3	78	0.6
1978	5	60	1.0
1979	4	351	0.7
1980	0	0	0.0
1981	4	4	0.7
1982	3	233	0.6
1983	4	15	0.8
1984	1	4	0.2
1985	4	197	0.7
1986	1	1	0.2

SAFETY OF SCHEDULED AIRLINE SERVICE

Source: U.S. Department of Transportation

There is more good news. Safety improvements continue to be made to planes. For example, one of the hidden hazards of flying is windshear, where dramatic changes in air currents can cause a pilot to lose control. Boeing has developed a windshear detector which it is now installing on new jetliners. In other areas, the Federal Aviation Administration recently required airlines to install more fire-retardant cushions, improve fire extinguishers and smoke detectors, and add emergency floor markings to help passengers escape dark, smoke-filled cabins.

Still, because of the rise in near-collisions, there is cause for concern. Reports of near-collisions increased from 478 in 1983, to 592 in 1984, to 785 in 1985. Nearly every day a major airline reports a problem that results in a diverted flight, an emergency landing, or a minor injury to a crew member or passenger. According to *The Wall Street Journal*, in one 90-day period in 1986, airlines reported 119 such incidents. Included were 11 fires, 18 instances of engine trouble, and seven problems concerning landing gears. One jet lost a wheel, two had windows break, and one flew in a direction exactly the opposite of the air traffic controller's instructions.

A number of factors may be responsible for any loss in safety.

Air and Airport Crowding: The number of flights in and out of U.S. airports has grown faster than airports themselves. This crowding is compounded by the increasing use of hub airports, where airlines concentrate a larger number of flights in a limited time period.

Fewer and Less Qualified Air Traffic Controllers: Five years after President Reagan fired members of the Air Traffic Controllers Union, PATCO, there were 13 percent fewer controllers. In addition, a significantly lower percentage of these controllers was considered fully qualified.

Less Experienced Pilots: The rising number of flights has forced some airlines to hire less experienced pilots from commuter lines. Furthermore, the increase in pilot movement between airlines has resulted in more crews unfamiliar with each other and with the equipment they operate.

Aging Planes: Despite new purchases by many airlines, the average age of all jetliners has increased. Like cars, the older the planes get, the more likely they are to break down. This places greater pressure on maintenance crews.

Declining Maintenance: Despite the growing need for proper plane maintenance, this servicing has declined. In the last few years, most major airlines have not increased their maintenance staff as rapidly as capacity has grown. This widening gap has been worsened by government cutbacks in safety inspectors and inspections. Between 1981 and 1984, the number of authorized inspectors declined by more than 20 percent. Actual inspections also fell.

Because of the growing concern about maintenance problems, the FAA has recently imposed hefty fines on several major airlines for inadequate maintenance. These penalties, however, have not stemmed the loss of public confidence in flying. Between 1970 and 1985, the proportion who believe air travel was safer than five years earlier fell from 60 percent to 16 percent. In 1985, 40 percent said it was actually less safe. The only slight comfort U.S. airlines can take is that, because of the threat of terrorism, the public fears overseas flying much more than domestic air travel.

MINIMIZING THE RISKS OF AIR TRAVEL

There are two ways to increase your flying safety. One pertains to flight selection, the other to cabin precautions.

Flight Selection: Airline travel is so much safer than most other transport that we are willing to fly any airline, anyplace, at any time. Those of you who are more nervous, however, may wish to avoid certain airlines, airports, and potentially hazardous weather conditions.

Safety Records: Some airlines have better safety records than others. In late 1985, *The Dallas Times Herald* published an analysis of pilot citations issued from 1980 to 1985. These violations ranged from disregarding air traffic control instructions, to flying at the wrong altitude, to improper training. Pilots at Continental, Midway, and American were ranked first, second, and third in total violations. Pilots at TWA, USAir, Frontier, and Pan American also had above average numbers of violations. Delta pilots had the lowest rate. Nevertheless, in 1987 Delta had a number of mishaps, some of which nearly caused collisions, suggesting that these statistics may not be an entirely reliable indicator of current performance.

Size of Aircraft: It is an established fact that you are safer flying on large jetliners than on small commuter planes. An analysis of safety records in the late 1970s indicates that passengers were about three times safer on the larger aircraft. This safety gap may have widened in the early 1980s because of the rising number of small plane accidents. In a five-month period, for example, the Provincetown-Boston Airline was involved in three fatal accidents. At the time, PBA was the nation's largest commuter airline. Also cause for concern are FAA charges that several commuter airlines, including PBA, have tried to cover up safety violations through false record-keeping.

Airport Factors: Contrary to conventional wisdom, it also appears safer to fly into major airports than into satellite fields. In 1987, *The Wall Street Journal* reported a higher near-collision rate at smaller airports. The article suggested that differences might reflect greater use by small planes and helicopters with less experienced pilots of, and more limited traffic control at, satellite airports. The following table compares near-collision rates.

NEAR COLLISION RATES (1986)	
Airport	Rate Per 100,000 Take-Offs and Landings
Chicago O'Hare	0.5
Chicago Midway	4.3
Houston International	0.0
Houston Hobby	3.6
Los Angeles International	1.2
Los Angeles – Long Beach	2.9
Los Angeles – Burbank	3.9
Los Angeles – Ontario	6.0
San Francisco International	0.5
San Jose	2.6
Oakland	1.6

Weather: Poor weather, especially thunderstorms and sleet, cause pilots to have less control of planes and rely more heavily on navigational instrumentation. One of the worst airplane accidents, the Air Florida crash in Washington D.C., appears to have been caused mainly by ice on an engine power sensor. One way to avoid bad weather is to make your reservations early, but wait until the day of the flight to purchase your ticket. Before you do, consult the weather report for all airports from which your plane is scheduled to take off or land.

Cabin Precautions: The following precautions can help you minimize the risk of death or injury in severe turbulence or a crash:

First, make certain no heavy or sharp items are stored in the bin over your head. If any are, request that they be moved. This is especially important for those sitting in aisle seats. A situation typical of the problem in this area was recently observed when a small, but hard and heavy, bag fell out of a bin, cutting and stunning a passenger in an aisle seat.

Second, fasten your seatbelt and, except when moving about in the plane, keep it fastened until the plane has come to a complete stop. Be sure you know how to open your seat belt quickly.

Third, pay attention to the safety briefing at the beginning of the flight. You may have heard most of it many times before, but possibly not information on the specific features of the aircraft. Pay special attention to the location of emergency exits because they vary from plane to plane. Also, read the safety instructions on the seat card.

Fourth, do not smoke in the restrooms or in the aisles. A tragic 1973 accident was caused by a burning cigarette in a washroom trash bin. Those smoking while standing could burn other passengers if the plane encounters turbulence.

Fifth, in the event of an emergency, listen to instructions from the flight crew. They are more likely than you to know what is happening. They also are trained to respond to crises.

Sixth, if your plane crash lands and you can move, get out of the plane as quickly as possible. Your greatest risk after the crash is from the smoke and deadly fumes from fires that may break out. These can overcome you in a minute or two. Since smoke rises, try to stay down and put a cloth over your nose and mouth.

12

PASSENGER HEALTH ✈
Cabin Hazards and How to Avoid Them

A far more common threat to the health of most air travelers than accidents is normal cabin conditions – motion, changes in air pressure, low humidity, inadequate circulation, tobacco smoke and other indoor air contaminants, and lack of medical services. This chapter documents cabin hazards and explains how to avoid or minimize them.

CABIN PRESSURE

The air pressure inside a typical high-flying plane is equal to the air pressure at an altitude of about 5,000 to 7,000 feet. This means air pressure is lower than what we are normally used to, and there is less oxygen in the cabin. As a result, gas trapped in bodily cavities expands and can cause discomfort. Wearing loose-fitting clothes, eating only small quantities of food, and avoiding carbonated beverages can all help make you more comfortable.

In addition, rapid changes in air pressure on take-off and especially on landing can be painful for those with colds, sinus infections, ear infections, and allergies that block Eustachian tubes. If you are suffering from any of these maladies, try to postpone your trip. If this is impossible, consider taking a decongestant an hour or so before descent. Once in the air, you can keep your Eustachian tubes open by swallowing or yawning frequently. In order to make it easier to swallow, many travelers chew gum or suck on candy.

A more drastic remedy is to unblock your ears by pinching

nostrils shut, taking a mouthful of air, and using only cheek and throat muscles, forcing air into the middle ear. A loud pop means you have succeeded. You may have to repeat this procedure several times during descent. Children who are unable intentionally to unblock ears may do so if they are sucking a bottle or pacifier.

After landing, if the ears fail to open or pain persists, consult a physician. He may need to release the pressure by probing the Eustachian tube or by making a small incision in the ear drum.

AIRSICKNESS

Less than one percent of flyers routinely suffer from motion sickness. But continued turbulence can make even the most hardened flyers nauseated. Keeping your head still and leaning it as far back as possible helps. So may an anti-seasickness drug taken an hour before take-off. As in the case of any drug, pregnant women should consult a doctor before taking these motion sickness pills.

If you are sensitive to turbulence, the best protection is to travel on large jetliners, not small commuter planes. The larger the aircraft, the greater the chance it will fly above the clouds and the worst turbulence. Large aircraft are also more stable in the air. Smaller planes fly at lower altitudes, often through clouds, and are bounced around by rough air.

LOW HUMIDITY

Humidity levels in planes are typically only 10 to 20 percent, well below comfort levels of 30 to 50 percent. This dryness, plus low cabin pressure, quickly causes a loss of body fluids and may lead to dehydration. The cure is to drink lots of water or fruit juices.

CABIN AIR POLLUTION

Airplane cabins are the most polluted environment to

which many people are exposed. While scientists are concerned about exposure to high levels of cosmic radiation, they are most worried about the contaminants trapped in cabins because of inadequate ventilation. If pilots turned on all ventilation systems, the ventilation rate in the coach section would be 20 cubic feet per passenger per minute. Yet, because they often operate these systems at two-thirds of capacity, the rate may dip below ten cubic feet per passenger per minute. The problem with these circulation rates is that on a typical flight with a full cabin and one-third of the passengers smoking, a ventilation rate of 50 to 75 is needed to alleviate irritation caused by smoke, according to one expert. This lack of adequate ventilation exposes passengers to a number of hazardous contaminants.

Secondary Smoke: The most noxious of these pollutants is secondary smoke from cigarettes. It is especially intolerable to those with respiratory disease, but it bothers many others as well. In one study of nonallergic persons exposed to secondary tobacco smoke, nearly 70 percent said they suffered eye irritation, 30 percent had nasal discomfort, 30 percent got headaches, and 25 percent developed coughs.

The DOT requires airlines to provide a seat in the non-smoking section to every passenger requesting one, as long as they meet the airline's deadline for arriving at the gate. In addition, cigar and pipe smoking is prohibited on all flights, and no smoking is allowed on aircraft with fewer than 30 seats. Smoking is also prohibited in lavatories, while standing or walking, and whenever the plane is on the ground.

Rather than waiting until you reach the gate to reserve a seat, request one far in advance away from the smoking areas in both first class and coach. This will help ensure that one is available. In the future, however, these early reservations may not be necessary to avoid exposure to secondary smoke on some flights. In 1987, the U.S. House of Representatives passed legislation forbidding smoking on all flights of less than two hours duration. Because the Surgeon-General has vigorously advocated this measure, passage by the Senate may lead to enactment of this measure.

Bacteria and Viruses: The other major cabin contaminants are bacteria and viruses. Although scientists have not conclusively proved that these pose a serious hazard, there is mounting evidence that this is the case. Often cited is the case of a 1978 flight from Alaska that sat for three hours with the ventilation system off. One of the 54 passengers on this plane had the flu. Within three days, nearly three-quarters of the passengers reported they had contracted a virus. Twenty of the 22 who were tested had evidence of a similar influenza infection.

Perhaps most convincing to us, however, is the frequency with which we come down with colds or the flu after flying. If there is such a link between flying and illness, it may also reflect factors such as the stress of traveling and depression of our immune systems by cosmic radiation.

To minimize exposure to all these pollutants while flying, take the following measures. First, as mentioned above, sit away from smoking areas. Second, open the air nozzle and aim it at your face. This will provide you with at least some fresh air. (It is not pure since, typically, about half represents recirculated air.) Third, if the cabin seems at all stuffy, inform a flight attendant and ask her to see that ventilation is increased. Particularly if others also complain, this may persuade the pilot to turn on the entire system or to switch it from low to high.

FOOD CONTAMINATION

In general, airline food is very safe. According to a Centers for Disease Control representative, since 1947 there have been only 20 known incidents of food poisoning on planes. Yet, recent U.S. Food and Drug Administration inspections of airline food storage revealed potential food hazards. In 1984, spot checks found examples of perishable foods being loaded on planes with little or no dry ice and stored at unsafe temperatures. More thorough investigation the following year revealed "serious potentially hazardous temperature problems" in 12 percent of inspections and less serious problems in another 23 percent. Nevertheless, these FDA concerns have not persuaded us to recommend giving up airline food for safety reasons.

JET LAG

Jet lag is the phenomenon that occurs when your "body time" is ahead or behind the actual time at your destination. It is a very real symptom. Because the body has an internal clock regulating daily habits, including sleeping, eating, and other functions, travelers crossing many time zones have the problem of conforming to the new zone against the body's natural instincts. On short trips, you should try as much as possible to keep to your home schedule. Despite the frustration of trying to get breakfast at 5:00 a.m. after flying from the East to the West Coast, we find this helps.

If remaining on the same schedule is not possible, consider the following measures. On the flight, eat lightly, drink lots of water or fruit juice (never much alcohol), and try to sleep. After arrival, consider taking a mild laxative to relieve constipation and a mild sedative to encourage sleep. Also, try to exercise before and after your flight, though because of possible lower resistance to infection, never overdo it.

WHEN NOT TO FLY

Certain physical conditions may pose a danger to air travelers. The American Medical Association recommends that those with the following conditions consult a physician before flying.

Advanced Pregnancy: Women pregnant beyond 240 days, or in danger of miscarriage, are at risk because the physiological and psychological stresses of flying may induce premature labor. Also, there might be considerable delays in securing adequate medical treatment.

Severe Respiratory Problems: Lower air pressure and rapid changes in pressure may endanger those with pneumothorax, lung cysts, severe lung disease, and acute sinusitis.

Cardiovascular Problems: Those who have had heart attacks within the previous four weeks or a stroke within two weeks, or who have uncontrolled hypertension or severe heart disease, may not survive the stress of flying or the lower oxygen content of cabin air.

Highly Contagious or Communicable Diseases: Those with infections and even skin diseases that could be passed on to other passengers should not fly.

A Wired Jaw: Those with fixed wiring for jaw fractures who become air sick could choke on their own vomit.

Other Ailments: Those with a recent skull fracture, a brain tumor, acute diverticulitis or ulcerative colitis, acute gastroenteritis, severe anemia, sickle cell disease, hemophilia with active bleeding, or recent eye surgery should consult a doctor before flying.

13

FLYING WITH CHILDREN
Ensuring Their (and Your) Comfort and Safety

With the increased availability of low fares and increasingly limited time for family vacations, more and more parents are traveling with children. While frequently characterized as one of parenting's worst experiences, flying with children can be fun.

This chapter describes ways to minimize the stress of traveling with children and offers suggestions for parents of children traveling alone.

CHILDREN IN THE AIR

Flying successfully with children requires care in everything from purchasing a ticket to packing for the flight. Here are some tips to make your next flight easier.

Making a Reservation: Minimizing problems begins when you purchase a ticket. First, try to select a nonstop flight, on a airline that reserves seats, during a time period when your children might be the most comfortable. For very young children who sleep well, that may be during nap time. For older children, who might enjoy the flight, that might mean early morning. Flying nonstop is important, not just because the flight will be shorter, but also because infants are especially sensitive to changes in cabin pressure during descent.

Second, try to reserve a seat behind a bulkhead. There is

more legroom and there are no seats in front of you. Since many airlines try to seat children in this row, there may be other parents and children nearby. Because young children are not allowed in rows with emergency exits, make sure you tell the reservations agent that you are traveling with children. Otherwise, you will have to change seats once on board.

Third, to guarantee that your child will be able to ride in a safety seat, you must pay for a separate ticket. (See safety seat information below.)

Fourth, if you are traveling with an infant, consider asking for a bassinet when you make your reservation. These cradles attach to the wall on a bulkhead or sit on the floor at your feet.

Packing for the Plane: Make certain to bring on board enough toys, food, drink, and diapers. Most airlines will not have the supplies you come to depend on when on the ground. If you are checking luggage, pack under the assumption you won't see your bags for several hours after landing.

Exactly what you carry on will depend on the age of your children. For infants and toddlers, diapers, wet wipes, clean clothes, and disposal bags are essential. Prepacked disposable bottles are more convenient than powdered or liquid concentrate. If your child uses a pacifier, it can help relieve the discomfort of changes in cabin pressure.

Carrying on enough food for toddlers and children is especially important. Because flight attendants must wait until the seat belt lights are turned off and they have served drinks, there is usually some delay before meals are served. This can be lengthened by delays in departure. In addition, because of the excitement of traveling, the metabolism of your children may increase, which means they may want to eat more than normal. For ease of clean-up, the simpler the better.

Most airlines carry a supply of children's entertainment kits – puzzles, coloring books, crayons, playing cards, and the like. But don't count on these being available. Tip: some parents reserve some special toys and books just for trips.

Boarding the Plane: Some parents give their children dramamine (motion-sickness medicine) or certain antihistamines to help keep their ear passages open and minimize the discomfort of cabin pressure changes. Before giving your children pre-flight medication, please consult your pediatrician. Usually airlines will ask those with small children to board first. If not, request that you be allowed to do so. This will give you enough time to seat your children, stow your gear, find pillows and blankets, refrigerate extra bottles, and cultivate flight attendants. Particularly if you have more than one child and the flight is a long one, the latter can prove invaluable.

In the Air: Since young children are more sensitive to changes in cabin pressure, give them something to drink or suck on during take-offs and landings. If you want to use the play packets offered by airlines, because they are in short supply, request them as soon as you board the plane. Many parents find that alternating activities – 20 minutes of play, then 20 minutes of reading – will help the time pass quickly for both of you. When the aisle is clear, a brief walk will help dissipate stored energy.

Ensuring Safety: The FAA requires that all airline passengers at least two years of age wear a seat belt during take off and landings. Parents have two options for those under two. They can hold children on their laps. Or they can supply their own FAA approved child safety seat.

Because the use of a safety seat may require the purchase of an extra ticket, most parents choose to hold infants. But this can be risky. In severe turbulence, a child may fall out of your arms. In a crash, he or she could hit the seat in front of you or be crushed in your arms. *Never* buckle your seat belt around both you and your child.

In order to guarantee that you can use a safety seat, you must purchase a second ticket. (Many airlines discount these 20 to 25 percent.) If there are vacant seats on the flight, most airlines will allow their free use. To guarantee an extra seat but minimize expense, reserve your tickets well in advance but wait until the last possible moment to purchase them. If the plane is full, you can buy two tickets. If it is not, you can purchase only one and get the free use of a vacant seat.

In order for a safety seat to be used on board, it must have an FAA approval sticker.

WHEN CHILDREN FLY ALONE

There may be a number of reasons why your child will need to take a trip alone. To ensure a safe, comfortable trip, plan carefully and well in advance. Also, make sure there is someone at the destination who will promptly pick up your child and call you to let you know of his arrival. Don't forget to send them off with their own "carry-on" bag of toys, puzzles, books, and snacks. Here are some things you should know in order to make it a smooth trip:

Age Restrictions: All major airlines require that children be at least five years old to fly alone. In addition, most require that young travelers be at least eight if the trip involves transfer to another airline. Children over twelve are generally considered able to take care of themselves, so receive no individual treatment unless a special arrangement is made with the airline.

Escort Service: Unless the traveler is a teenager with experience flying and assuming responsibility, we recommend hiring the airline escort service, especially if there is a connection. Most major airlines offer this service for children up to 17. This includes assistance with boarding, quick attention to their needs while flying, an escort during transfers, and an escort at the destination until met. TWA in St. Louis and New York (John F. Kennedy) has a special child care center where children can read, watch TV, or play games. Airlines charge $20 per trip, or $40 for a round-trip. This service must be arranged with the airline in advance. At check-in, you must fill out some forms and pay the fee. At this time, also check the ticket, boarding pass, and claim checks to ensure their accuracy. Remind your child to keep them in a safe place and only give them to airline agents.

At the Gate: Make certain that the child has cash for emergencies and clear identification with names and phone numbers to call if problems arise. Remind him or her of the importance of not leaving the airport until picked up and of how to seek help if nobody is waiting.

Once your child has boarded, do not leave the gate until the plane has taken off. If he is "trapped" on a plane that never gets off the ground, you will want to be there when it returns to the gate.

The U.S. Department of Transportation has prepared a useful pamphlet entitled *Children and Teens in Flight*, available from DOT's Office of Consumer Affairs Department I-25, 400 Seventh Street, SW, Washington, D.C. 20590. Its most useful feature is a travel card that allows you to send important information about the flight, and adult contact persons, with the child.

14

SPECIAL NEEDS
Suggestions for the Disabled Traveler

I n the past decade, disabled people have gained greater access to air travel. Today the Federal Aviation Administration requires each airline to have for their review a policy for treating disabled passengers. Moreover, the federal government has insisted that any airports built with any government funds have barrier-free facilities. Consequently, for most people with disabilities, air travel does not pose the insurmountable obstacles it once did.

Nevertheless, flying for the disabled traveler is not always easy. Policies and services vary from airline to airline. Furthermore, some people with disabilities still complain about discrimination, for example, the refusal of airlines to allow the blind to sit next to emergency exits. As a result, it is very important for the disabled to make careful preparations. This chapter will help these preparations by explaining how to plan for a trip, how to select an airline, how to book a flight, what to do at the airport, how to board the plane, and what to do during the flight.

PLANNING THE TRIP

In planning their trip, people with disabilities must know whether they will be allowed to travel alone, what equipment or seeing eye dogs they can bring, and what restrictions apply to stretcher passengers.

Need For a Companion: Generally, passengers who

cannot feed themselves or care for their personal hygiene must be accompanied by an attendant during the flight. So must stretcher passengers.

Blind Passengers: Of all disabled travelers, blind persons are easiest for the airlines to assist. They may sit anywhere they like in the cabin except near an emergency exit. They may also travel with a seeing eye dog, which rides for free at their feet.

Wheelchairs: It is advisable to avoid traveling with battery-operated wheelchairs. If absolutely necessary, new FAA regulations apply: wheelchairs with non-spillable batteries may be carried as checked baggage if the battery is disconnected, the terminals are insulated to prevent short circuits, and the battery is securely attached to the chair. Wheelchairs with spillable batteries may be carried as checked baggage if the chair can be boarded, stored, secured, and unloaded always in an upright position. The battery must be disconnected, the terminals insulated to prevent short circuits, and the battery securely attached. Otherwise, a spillable battery must be removed from the chair and packed for storage.

Oxygen: Carrying on oxygen is subject to FAA regulations. If you have a battery-powered respirator, you must inform the airline in advance. They may supply oxygen (for a charge) but are not required to. You may bring your own oxygen into the cabin only if it has been supplied by a firm, such as Air Medic, that packs according to FAA specifications. You must also receive airline approval to do so. The FAA advises using the airline's oxygen, if available, and shipping your own as cargo. In fact, most major airlines permit oxygen use in flight but require use of the airline's own supply. For this service there is typically a $50 charge and an advance notification requirement (ranging from 24 to 72 hours).

SELECTING A FLIGHT

In selecting a flight, the disabled should consider specific airline policies and the availability of aircraft especially suited to their travel needs. The table below contains information on airline policies. As can be seen, there are some differences as to when major airlines require a medical certificate and a companion. There are, however, even greater differences in their provision of oxygen and treatment of stretcher passengers.

Six major airlines transport stretcher passengers, but Eastern, Piedmont, and United will not. All that do, however, require the purchase of three to nine seats, often in first class.

Several airlines have purchased Boeing 767s that are specially configured for wheelchairs. These planes have a lavatory accessible to on-board wheelchairs. It features an oversized door, low-entry threshold, built-in assist devices, a lowered door latch, lever handles for toilets and doors, and increased floor space. In addition, there is a ten square foot private area adjacent to the lavatory that can be used for maneuvering or by a companion. The plane also has four seats with movable armrests – two in first class, two in coach – for easier transfer between aisle chair and passenger seat. United, American, Delta, TWA, and Alaska have purchased some of these aircraft.

Other airlines have planes with special features useful to the disabled. Some seats on Eastern's 727s have folding armrests, and all seats on their A300s and B757s have them. The B757 also has an assist rail in one coach lavatory. Piedmont is planning to acquire a Manten Chair, which eliminates the need to transfer a non-ambulatory passenger from one chair to another when making flight connections.

AIRLINE POLICIES REGARDING DISABLED PASSENGERS	
Airline	**Policies**
Continental	**Advance Notice Required for Oxygen Use:** Not allowed **Must Use Airline's Oxygen:** N/A **Stretcher Passengers Accepted:** Yes **Number of Seats Required for Stretchers:** 4 **Medical Certificate Required When:** Passenger on stretcher or seriously ill **Companion Required When:** Passenger on stretcher or not self-sufficient
Delta	**Advance Notice Required for Oxygen Use:** 24 hours **Must Use Airline's Oxygen:** Yes **Stretcher Passengers Accepted:** Yes **Required Seat Purchase for Stretchers:** 3 first class **Medical Certificate Required When:** Passenger just out of hospital, needs oxygen, or seriously ill **Companion Required When:** Passenger paraplegic, double amputee, or not self-sufficient
Eastern	**Advance Notice Required for Oxygen Use:** 48 hours **Must Use Airline's Oxygen:** Yes **Stretcher Passengers Accepted:** No **Required Seat Purchase for Stretchers:** N/A **Medical Certificate Required When:** Passenger ambulatory and unaccompanied **Companion Required When:** Passenger not self-sufficient

AIRLINE POLICIES REGARDING DISABLED PASSENGERS

Airline	Policies
Northwest	**Advance Notice Required for Oxygen Use:** 48 hours **Must Use Airline's Oxygen:** Yes **Stretcher Passengers Accepted:** Yes **Required Seat Purchase for Stretchers:** 3-4 first class **Medical Certificate Required When:** Case by case **Companion Required When:** Passenger not self-sufficient
Pan American	**Advance Notice Required for Oxygen Use:** 48 hours **Must Use Airline's Oxygen:** No **Stretcher Passengers Accepted:** Yes **Required Seat Purchase for Stretchers:** 9 **Medical Certificate Required When:** Passenger needs oxygen and case by case **Companion Required When:** Passenger not self-sufficient
Piedmont	**Advance Notice Required for Oxygen Use:** 48 hours **Must Use Airline's Oxygen:** No **Stretcher Passengers Accepted:** No **Required Seat Purchase for Stretchers:** N/A **Medical Certificate Required When:** Case by case **Companion Required When:** Passenger not self-sufficient

AIRLINE POLICIES REGARDING DISABLED PASSENGERS

Airline	Policies
TWA	**Advance Notice Required for Oxygen Use:** 72 hours **Must Use Airline's Oxygen:** Yes **Stretcher Passengers Accepted:** Yes **Required Seat Purchase for Stretchers:** 4 first class **Medical Certificate Required When:** Case by case **Companion Required When:** Passenger not self-sufficient
United	**Advance Notice Required for Oxygen Use:** 72 hours **Must Use Airline's Oxygen:** Yes **Stretcher Passengers Accepted:** No **Required Seat Purchase for Stretchers:** N/A **Medical Certificate Required When:** Passenger nonstatic ambulatory or non-ambulatory **Companion Required When:** Case by case
USAir	**Advance Notice Required for Oxygen Use:** 72 hours **Must Use Airline's Oxygen:** No **Stretcher Passengers Accepted:** Yes **Required Seat Purchase for Stretchers:** 3 **Medical Certificate Required When:** Passenger in ninth month of pregnancy **Companion Required When:** Passenger deaf-blind

BOOKING THE FLIGHT

Because of the complexities of traveling with a disability, it is wise to seek the assistance of an experienced travel agent. A trade association called the Society for the Advancement of Travel for the Handicapped (126 Court Street, Brooklyn, NY 11242; 718-858-5483) can refer you to a travel agent capable of addressing special travel needs.

Advance Notice: Whether you use an agent or make the booking yourself, do this well in advance of the flight. This allows time to work out any problems, increases the chance of getting a preferred seat, and minimizes the risk to wheelchair travelers of being denied a ticket. Airlines frequently limit the number of these passengers to four or five. In any event, do not wait to make reservations until the last minute. Some airlines will not sell you a ticket within 48 hours of the flight.

Communications by the Deaf and Hearing Impaired: Deaf and hearing impaired passengers may make reservations with many airlines by calling special TDD phone numbers. These numbers are:

American		800-543-1586
Eastern		800-325-3553
Northwest		800-328-2298
Pan American		800-722-3322
Piedmont		800-334-5874
TWA		800-421-8480
	(CA only)	800-252-0622
United		800-323-0170
	(IL only)	800-942-8519
USAir		800-245-2966

Information Needed by Airline: Disabled travelers making reservations should supply the following information to the airline.

- The nature of the disability, whether the passenger uses crutches or a wheelchair, and whether the wheelchair is electrically powered

- Whether help is needed alighting from or entering vehicles at the airport, or getting from the parking area to the terminal
- Whether assistance is needed to board or leave the plane
- Whether help is needed to use the lavatory
- Any special dietary requests and need for assistance at meals
- Whether assistance is needed with checking in or checking out luggage
- Whether another person will accompany the disabled traveler
- Any seating preference

Seat Selection: Wheelchair travelers should request a front row aisle seat. There is more aisle space here for maneuvering the chair. All other disabled travelers should also consider asking for a first row seat. These are easiest to get to and are often close to flight attendants. Blind persons may wish to request a window seat behind the bulkhead. There is room in this row for a seeing eye dog, and sitting by the window will give others in the row unrestricted access to the aisle.

NEGOTIATING THE AIRPORT

If you have requested assistance, arrive at the airport early, perhaps an hour before departure. This will allow adequate time to obtain help, clear security, and board the plane. For a free booklet describing design features at major airports that are important to the disabled, write to Consumer Information Center, Department 571T, Pueblo, CO 81009 and ask for *Access Travel: Airports*, published by the Airport Operators International Council.

Clearing Security: If you need a wheelchair at the terminal entrance or check-in counter, it will be provided. After check-in, you must clear a security checkpoint. Many disabled travelers will not want to pass through the metal detectors because their equipment will set off the alarm. These include people riding in wheelchairs, using metal canes or crutches for support, or wearing braces, artificial limbs, a pacemaker, or hearing aids. These persons should request an inspection by hand. In addition, if you are carrying expensive or fragile equipment, do not risk damaging it by allowing x-ray examination. Instead, request a hand inspection.

Boarding the Plane: Almost all airlines board those needing assistance first. But as a precaution, when you arrive at the gate, ask if you will be able to do so. This is especially important for blind persons since airlines do not officially classify them as handicapped, even though many insist on boarding unaccompanied blind people in a wheelchair.

For those in wheelchairs, boarding is always easiest if there is a jetway or mobile lounge. When there is, you will probably be allowed to be wheeled to the door of the plane in your wheelchair. Boarding at small airports or on small planes, however, may be more complicated. Most airlines can supply a high-backed chair especially constructed to enter the door and move down aisles of planes smaller than jumbo jets. If there is not a jetway, you may be pushed up a ramp in a boarding chair, carried up a flight of steps, or lifted on a forklift device. Major airports are required to have the latter. There is also a new type of boarding chair with a climbing mechanism in which the chair itself climbs the steps. TWA has developed a vehicle called a Handicapped Lift for use in terminals without jetways. This is an enclosed elevator-type unit that can move two wheelchairs and an operator at the same time.

Your wheelchair will always ride in the baggage compartment. But if you need it soon after arriving at your destination, you can get an "escort ticket" that indicates you will need it after landing. Many airlines will place your chair in baggage last so that it will be the first item unloaded. Some airlines recommend that you purchase a bicycle container at the airport to ensure its protection. At the destination, power wheelchairs will usually be delivered to the baggage area, while manual chairs may be brought to the plane.

IN THE PLANE

Wheelchair Passengers: On the plane you may sit in

a special seat with an armrest that permits easy access. If you use metal or wooden canes or crutches that are not collapsible, you will have to relinquish them for safe stowing. They will be returned to you before leaving the plane. Because of their size and design, lavatories on most planes are not accessible to passengers in wheelchairs. Those riding in these aircraft should use the facilities at the airport before departure. As mentioned earlier, however, a few new planes, such as the Boeing 767, have accessible lavatories and on-board wheelchairs to carry you there.

Blind Passengers: Many airlines will give blind travelers pre-flight briefings on emergency evacuation procedures, location of oxygen masks, and other features of the cabin and cabin service. Those using fiber-glass, metal, or wooden canes that fold or collapse may keep them under their seats, provided they can be stowed without protruding.

Hearing-Impaired Passengers: Deaf and hearing-impaired flyers should remember that most hearing aids do not usually operate effectively on planes because of the background noise of the engines. Also, most flight attendants do not understand sign language or finger spelling. Thus, the hearing-impaired should keep a pad and pencil to facilitate communication. Many airlines permit hearing-ear dogs to travel at the feet of their owners.

15

COMPLAINTS
How to Resolve Them

Surprisingly, air travelers have very few rights when it comes to complaints and problems with service. This chapter explains how those with complaints can maximize their chances of getting satisfaction.

Given the limited leverage of airline travelers, the best complaint strategy is a preventive one. Try to avoid those situations where problems are likely to arise. Previous chapters contain dozens of specific recommendations for minimizing these risks. These suggestions range from flying during off-peak hours, to arriving at the airport well before scheduled departures, to carrying bags onto the plane.

Even when these preventive strategies are pursued, however, problems often arise. As a general rule, take immediate action. At the airport, ask to see the customer service representative who has authority to resolve grievances. They can arrange meals and hotel rooms for stranded passengers, write checks for denied boarding compensation, or arrange luggage repairs. If your luggage is lost or stolen, it is essential to file a complaint before you leave the airport.

Away from the airport, ask a customer contact person handling calls for reservations and ticketing information for the name and number of the appropriate airline representative to handle your complaint. Better yet, if you have done much business with your travel agent, ask him or her to try to resolve the problem.

If you are unable to resolve your complaint quickly, the odds are against your getting satisfaction. There are two useful pamphlets which summarize your rights: *Fly-Rights: A*

Guide to Air Travel in the U.S. is available free from the Consumer Affairs Division, Room 10405, Intergovernmental and Consumer Affairs, U.S. Department of Transportation, 400 Seventh St., S W, Washington, D.C. 20590, and *Facts and Advice for Airline Passengers* is available from Aviation Consumer Action Project, P.O. Box 19029, Washington, D.C. 20036 for $2.

If you are protected by one of these rights, such as reimbursement for lost luggage, you should pursue your complaint. If unable to resolve the grievance by phone, we suggest you call the U.S. Department of Transportation complaint hotline at 202-366-2220. They will take information about your complaint over the phone, communicate it to the airline, and include it in monthly complaint statistics.

If the airline still does not resolve your grievance, consider filing it with an office of a state or local consumer protection agency. If you are uncertain where to turn here, call City Hall or the state attorney general's office. While a few agencies will allow you to file complaints by phone, most require a written description. Keep this as short and objective as possible. Include all relevant facts – airline, dates, even airline service personnel with whom you dealt. Finally, send copies of relevant documents like tickets or receipts.

If this proves unsuccessful, as a last resort you can file a complaint with your local small claims court. This does not require the assistance of an attorney. In most cases, the amount of your request for settlement will be well within the court's limit, typically $1,500. It is helpful to submit the same information you gave to a protection agency. At a hearing, you will have an opportunity to summarize these documents in the presence of the airline's representative(s). Keep in mind, however, that collecting a small claims judgment can be frustrating, demanding additional time and even expense.

If you are not protected by an airline right, file a grievance anyway with DOT. They will pass it on to the airline and include it in their monthly statistical report. Should you also write to the airline? Such a communication certainly does no harm and may have therapeutic value to you, but it probably won't resolve your problem.

16

AIRLINE PROFILES

The tables on the following pages profile the specific offerings of each of the major airlines.

We have included a list of states that each airline serves, types of discount fares available, advance purchase requirements, frequent flyer plans, and credit cards accepted.

The tables also provide information on ticketing and refunds, which includes information on the *Bumping Comp. Deadline*. In order to be compensated for an airline "bumping" you (denying you boarding because they oversold the flight), you must be at the gate by the time indicated in the table. We also provide information on charges associated with lost tickets and delay time you can expect on ticket refunds.

Seating information, including how far in advance you can make a reservation for a specific seat, is also included.

The baggage section of each table tells how much free baggage you can take along and how much you will have to pay if you are over the airline's limit.

The profiles also list which special meals are available and how long in advance you need to order those meals. We have also included some specific tips for disabled travelers.

If you are traveling with a pet, consult the tables to determine what the airlines charge for kennels and how much advance notice is required.

Finally, the section on children includes information on how old they have to be to travel alone and to change planes, and what kinds of discounts are available.

KEY TO THE AIRLINE PROFILE CHARTS

To make the following tables easier to use, we have abbreviated some of the information. The following is a key to understanding the tables.

Fare Discounts

FA	=	Family
MI	=	Military
RM	=	Retired Military
SR	=	Senior Citizen
ST	=	Student

Credit Cards

AE	=	American Express
CB	=	Carte Blanche
DC	=	Diners Club
DI	=	Discover
MC	=	Mastercard
VI	=	Visa

Types of Meals

CH	=	Children's
DI	=	Diabetic
GF	=	Gluten-Free
HN	=	Hindu Non-Vegetarian
HV	=	Hindu Vegetarian
HY	=	Hypoglycemic
KO	=	Kosher
LCA	=	Low Calorie
LCH	=	Low Cholesterol
LS	=	Low Sodium
MO	=	Moslem
SF	=	Seafood
SR	=	Special Requests
VE	=	Vegetarian with Eggs/Milk
VP	=	Vegetarian Pure

AIR WISCONSIN

Availability
States served: IA, IL, IN, KY, MD, MI, OH, PA, RI, VA, WI

Fares
Discount Fares:	FA, MI, SR
Advance Purchase Req.:	7, 2 days
Holiday blackouts:	Yes
Frequent flyer plan:	Yes, U.S. only
Credit cards accepted:	AE, DC, MC, VI

Ticketing and Refunds
Bumping comp. deadline:	10 minutes
Lost ticket charge:	$30.00
Min. delay on refund ticket:	3 months

Seating
Advance seat reservation:	Yes, 360 days

Baggage
Pieces of free baggage:	3 pieces, 70 lbs.
Cost per extra bag:	$10.00 each
Lost baggage claims period:	45 days

Meals
Special meals available:	DI, KO, LC, LCH, LS, SF
Latest time to order:	24 hours advance notice

Disabled Passengers
Aisle boarding chair:	Yes
Wheelchair quota:	No
Seeing eye dog:	Yes
Hearing dog:	Yes
Oxygen:	No
TDD service:	Yes

Pets	
Charge for kennel:	$15.00-$70.00
Advance notice required:	24 hours advance notice
Children	
Min. age to travel alone:	5
Min. age to change planes:	8
Discount available w/adult:	Yes
Discount available alone:	No
Maximum age for discount:	11
Amount of discount:	20% excursion

ALASKA

Availability
States served: AK, AZ, CA, DC, ID, IL, NV, OR, TX, WA

Fares
Discount Fares: MI, SR
Advance Purchase Req.: 30, 14, 7, 2 days
Holiday blackouts: No
Frequent flyer plan: Yes
Credit cards accepted: AE, CB, DC, DI, MC, VI

Ticketing and Refunds
Bumping comp. deadline: 10 minutes
Lost ticket charge: $30.00
Min. delay on refund ticket: 4 months

Seating
Advance seat reservation: Yes, 28 days

Baggage
Pieces of free baggage: 2 pieces, 70 lbs.
Cost per extra bag: $15.00 each
Lost baggage claims period: 45 days

Meals
Special meals available: CH, DI, HY, KO, LCA, LCH, LS, SF, VE, VP
Latest time to order: 4 hours advance notice

Disabled Passengers

Aisle boarding chair:	Yes
Wheelchair quota:	No
Seeing eye dog:	Yes
Hearing dog:	Yes
Oxygen:	Yes, carrier supply only, advance notice
TDD service:	No

Pets

Charge for kennel:	$20.00-$45.00
Advance notice required:	24 hours advance notice

Children

Min. age to travel alone:	5
Min. age to change planes:	8
Discount available w/adult:	Yes
Discount available alone:	No
Maximum age for discount:	11
Amount of discount:	25% of published fare

ALOHA

Availability
States served:	HI

Fares
Discount Fares:	MI, SR
Advance Purchase Req.:	No
Holiday blackouts:	No
Frequent flyer plan:	Yes
Credit cards accepted:	AE, CB, DC, MC, VI

Ticketing and Refunds
Bumping comp. deadline:	10 minutes
Lost ticket charge:	$10.00
Min. delay on refund ticket:	4 months

Seating
Advance seat reservation:	Yes, 331 days

Baggage
Pieces of free baggage:	2 pieces, 70 lbs.
Cost per extra bag:	$10.00 each
Lost baggage claims period:	45 days

Meals
Special meals available:	No
Latest time to order:	N/A

Disabled Passengers
Aisle boarding chair:	Yes
Wheelchair quota:	Yes
Seeing eye dog:	Yes
Hearing dog:	Yes
Oxygen:	Yes, carriers supply, advance notice
TDD service:	

Pets	
Charge for kennel:	$15.00-$20.00
Advance notice required:	24 hours advance notice
Children	
Min. age to travel alone:	5
Min. age to change planes:	8
Discount available w/adult:	YES
Discount available alone:	YES
Maximum age for discount:	11
Amount of discount:	N/A

AMERICAN

Availability

States served:	AL, AK, AR, AZ, CA, CO, DC, FL, GA, HA, IA, IL, IN, KS, KY, LA, MD, MA, MI, MN, MS, MO, NE, NV, NJ, NM, NY, NC, OH, OK, OR, PA, RI SC, TN, TX, UT, VA, WA, WI

Fares

Discount Fares:	FM, MI, SC
Advance Purchase Req.:	30, 14, 7 days
Holiday blackouts:	Yes
Frequent flyer plan:	Yes
Credit cards accepted:	AE, CB, DC, DI, MC, VI

Ticketing and Refunds

Bumping comp. deadline:	5 minutes
Lost ticket charge:	$35.00
Min. delay on refund ticket:	3 months

Seating

Advance seat reservation:	Yes, 1 year

Baggage

Pieces of free baggage:	3 pieces, 70 lbs.
Cost per extra bag:	$30.00 each
Lost baggage claims period:	21 days

Meals

Special meals available:	CH, DI, HY, HV, KO, LCA, LCH, LS, MO, SF, VP
Latest time to order:	KO-12 hrs, Others-6 hrs advance notice

Disabled Passengers

Aisle boarding chair:	Yes
Wheelchair quota:	Yes, limited
Seeing eye dog:	Yes
Hearing dog:	Yes
Oxygen:	Yes, carriers supply, advance Reservation & medical approval
TDD service:	Yes

Pets

Charge for kennel:	$14-70
Advance notice required:	2 weeks advance notice

Children

Min. age to travel alone:	5
Min. age to change planes:	8
Discount available w/adult:	Yes
Discount available alone:	No
Maximum age for discount:	12
Amount of discount:	33%

AMERICA WEST

Availability
States served: AZ, CA, CT, CO, IA, IL, KS, MD, MO

NE, NM, NV, NY, OR, TX, UT, WA

Fares
Discount Fares:	No
Advance Purchase Req.:	14, 7, 2 days
Holiday blackouts:	Yes
Frequent flyer plan:	Yes
Credit cards accepted:	AE, CB, DC, DI, MC, VI

Ticketing and Refunds
Bumping comp. deadline:	10 minutes
Lost ticket charge:	$20.00
Min. delay on refund ticket:	4-6 weeks

Seating
Advance seat reservation:	Yes, 4 hours

Baggage
Pieces of free baggage:	3 pieces, 70 lbs.
Cost per extra bag:	$10.00 each
Lost baggage claims period:	45 days

Meals
Special meals available:	KO
Latest time to order:	24 hours advance notice

Disabled Passengers
Aisle boarding chair:	Yes
Wheelchair quota:	No
Seeing eye dog:	Yes
Hearing dog:	Yes
Oxygen:	No
TDD service:	No

Pets	
Charge for kennel:	N/A
Advance notice required:	N/A

Children	
Min. age to travel alone:	5
Min. age to change planes:	7
Discount available w/adult:	No
Discount available alone:	No
Maximum age for discount:	11
Amount of discount:	Varies, published fares

BRANIFF

Availability
States served:	AZ, CA, DC, FL, IL, MA, MD, MI, MO, NV, NY, TX, VA, WA

Fares
Discount Fares:	MI, SR, ST
Advance Purchase Req.:	14, 7, 2 days
Holiday blackouts:	No
Frequent flyer plan:	No
Credit cards accepted:	AE, CB, DC, DI, MC, VI

Ticketing and Refunds
Bumping comp. deadline:	10 minutes
Lost ticket charge:	$30.00
Min. delay on refund ticket:	6 months

Seating
Advance seat reservation:	Yes, 330 days

Baggage
Pieces of free baggage:	3 pieces, 70 lbs.
Cost per extra bag:	$10.00 each
Lost baggage claims period:	45 days

Meals
Special meals available:	KO
Latest time to order:	No notice required

Disabled Passengers

Aisle boarding chair:	Yes
Wheelchair quota:	No
Seeing eye dog:	Yes
Hearing dog:	Yes
Oxygen:	Yes, 48 hours advance notice, companion required, medical certificate
TDD service:	No

Pets

Charge for kennel:	$25.00-$65.00
Advance notice required:	No

Children

Min. age to travel alone:	5
Min. age to change planes:	8
Discount available w/adult:	Yes
Discount available alone:	Yes
Maximum age for discount:	17
Amount of discount:	25%

CONTINENTAL

Availability
States served: AK, AZ, CA, CO, CT, DC, FL, GA, HI, IA, IL, IN, KY, LA, MA, MD, ME, MI, MN, MO, MS, MT, NC, ND, NH, NJ, NM, NV, NY, OH, OK, OR, PA, RI, SC, SD, TN, TX, UT, VA, VT, WA, WI, WV

Fares
Discount Fares:	MI, SR, ST
Advance Purchase Req.:	7, 2 days
Holiday blackouts:	Yes
Frequent flyer plan:	Yes
Credit cards accepted:	AE, CB, DI, MC, VI

Ticketing and Refunds
Bumping comp. deadline:	10 minutes
Lost ticket charge:	$35
Min. delay on refund ticket:	25 days

Seating
Advance seat reservation:	Yes, 18 days

Baggage
Pieces of free baggage:	3 pieces, 70 lbs.
Cost per extra bag:	$30 each
Lost baggage claims period:	60 days

Meals
Special meals available:	HV, KO, MO, LS, SR = Infant, VE, VP
Latest time to order:	24 hours advance notice

Disabled Passengers

Aisle boarding chair:	Yes, carry service
Wheelchair quota:	No
Seeing eye dog:	Yes
Hearing dog:	Yes
Oxygen:	No
TDD service:	No

Pets

Charge for kennel:	$30-55
Advance notice required:	24 hours advance notice

Children

Min. age to travel alone:	5
Min. age to change planes:	8
Discount available w/adult:	Yes
Discount available alone:	Yes, 12-17
Maximum age for discount:	17
Amount of discount:	Varies

DELTA

Availability
States served: AL, AK, AR, AZ, CA, CO, CT, DC, FL, GA, HI, ID, IL, IN, KY, LA, MA, MD, ME, MI, MN, MO, MS, MT, NE, NC, ND, NJ, NM, NV, NY, OH, OK, OR, PA, SC, SD, TN, TX, UT, VA, WA, WY

Fares
Discount Fares:	FA, MI, SR, ST
Advance Purchase Req.:	7, 2 days
Holiday blackouts:	Yes
Frequent flyer plan:	Yes
Credit cards accepted:	AE, CB, DI, DC, MC, VI

Ticketing and Refunds
Bumping comp. deadline:	10 minutes
Lost ticket charge:	$35.00
Min. delay on refund ticket:	1-3 months

Seating
Advance seat reservation:	Yes, 31 days

Baggage
Pieces of free baggage:	3 pieces, 70 lbs.
Cost per extra bag:	$30.00 each
Lost baggage claims period:	21 days

Meals
Special meals available:	CH, DI, KO, LCA, LCH, LS, MO, SF, SR = infant, toddler, low-fat, bland, fruit, VE, VP
Latest time to order:	8 hours advance notice

Disabled Passengers	
Aisle boarding chair:	Yes
Wheelchair quota:	Yes
Seeing eye dog:	Yes
Hearing dog:	Yes
Oxygen:	Yes, 24 hours advance notice
TDD service:	Yes

Pets	
Charge for kennel:	$35.00-$70.00
Advance notice required:	24 hours advance notice

Children	
Min. age to travel alone:	5
Min. age to change planes:	8
Discount available w/adult:	Yes
Discount available alone:	No
Maximum age for discount:	11-17
Amount of discount:	Varies

EASTERN

Availability

States served: AL, AZ, CA, CO, CT, DC, DE, FL, GA, IL, IN, KY, LA, MA, MI, MN, MO, MS, NC, NJ, NV, NM, NY, OH, OK, OR, PA, RI, SC, TN, TX, UT, VA, WA, WI

Fares

Discount Fares: SR, MI, ST, FA
Advance Purchase Req.: 30, 14, 7, 2 days
Holiday blackouts: Yes
Frequent flyer plan: Yes
Credit cards accepted: AE, CB, DC, DI, MC, VI

Ticketing and Refunds

Bumping comp. deadline: 10 minutes
Lost ticket charge: $35.00
Min. delay on refund ticket: 3 months

Seating

Advance seat reservation: Yes, 31 days

Baggage

Pieces of free baggage: 3 pieces, 70 lbs.
Cost per extra bag: $25.00 each
Lost baggage claims period: 21 days

Meals

Special meals available: CH, DI, GF, HN, HV, HY, KO, LCA, LCH, LS, MO, SF, SR, VE, VP
Latest time to order: 8 hours advance notice

Disabled Passengers

Aisle boarding chair:	Yes
Wheelchair quota:	Yes
Seeing eye dog:	Yes
Hearing dog:	Yes
Oxygen:	Yes, carriers supply, medically Approved
TDD service:	No

Pets

Charge for kennel:	$15.00-$50.00
Advance notice required:	24 hours advance notice
Min. age to travel alone:	5
Min. age to change planes:	8
Discount available w/adult:	Yes
Discount available alone:	No
Maximum age for discount:	11-17
Amount of discount:	Varies

HAWAIIAN

Availability
States served: AK, CA, HI, NV, OR, WA, AMERICAN SOMOA

Fares
Discount Fares: FA, MI, SR, ST
Advance Purchase Req.: 14, 7 days
Holiday blackouts: Yes
Frequent flyer plan: Yes
Credit cards accepted: AE, MC, CB, VI, DC

Ticketing and Refunds
Bumping comp. deadline: 10 minutes
Lost ticket charge: No
Min. delay on refund ticket: 1-2 months

Seating
Advance seat reservation: Yes, 48 hours-21 days

Baggage
Pieces of free baggage: 2 pieces, 70 lbs.
Cost per extra bag: $10.00 each
Lost baggage claims period: 45 days

Meals
Special meals available: CH, DI, HV, KO, LCA, LCH, LS, SF, VE, VP
Latest time to order: 24 hours advance notice

Disabled Passengers

Aisle boarding chair:	Yes
Wheelchair quota:	N/A
Seeing eye dog:	Yes
Hearing dog:	Yes
Oxygen:	Yes, advance notice, service charge
TDD service:	N/A

Pets

Charge for kennel:	$20.00-$25.00
Advance notice required:	No

Children

Min. age to travel alone:	5
Min. age to change planes:	5
Discount available w/adult:	Yes
Discount available alone:	Yes, inter-island
Maximum age for discount:	11
Amount of discount:	25%

MIDWAY

Availability
States served: AZ, CO, DC, FL, IA, IL, IN, LA, MA, MI, MN, MO, NE, NV, NY, OH, PA, TX, US VIRGIN ISLANDS

Fares
Discount Fares:	MI, ST, FA
Advance Purchase Req.:	14, 7, 1 days
Holiday blackouts:	No
Frequent flyer plan:	Yes
Credit cards accepted:	AE, CB, DC, DI, MC, VI

Ticketing and Refunds
Bumping comp. deadline:	10 minutes
Lost ticket charge:	$25.00
Min. delay on refund ticket:	4 months

Seating
Advance seat reservation:	Yes, 30 days

Baggage
Pieces of free baggage:	3 pieces, 70 lbs.
Cost per extra bag:	$15.00 each
Lost baggage claims period:	45 days

Meals
Special meals available:	SNACKS ONLY, KO, LS, VE, VP
Latest time to order:	48 hours advance notice

Disabled Passengers

Aisle boarding chair:	Yes
Wheelchair quota:	No
Seeing eye dog:	Yes
Hearing dog:	Yes
Oxygen:	No
TDD service:	No

Pets

Charge for kennel:	$30.00
Advance notice required:	24 hours advance notice, subject to space

Children

Min. age to travel alone:	5
Min. age to change planes:	8
Discount available w/adult:	Yes
Discount available alone:	No
Maximum age for discount:	11-17
Amount of discount:	Varies

NORTHWEST

Availability

States served: AK, AL, AR, AZ, CA, CO, CT, DC, DE, FL, GA, HI, IA, IL, IN, KS, LA, MA, MD, MI, MN, MO, MS, MT, ND, NE, NJ, NV, OH, OK, OR, PA, RI, SD, TN, TX, UT, WA, WI, WY

Fares

Discount Fares:	MI
Advance Purchase Req.:	30, 14, 7, 2 days
Holiday blackouts:	Yes
Frequent flyer plan:	Yes
Credit cards accepted:	AE, CB, DC, DI, MC, VI

Ticketing and Refunds

Bumping comp. deadline:	10 minutes
Lost ticket charge:	$50
Min. delay on refund ticket:	3 months

Seating

Advance seat reservation:	Yes, Not Frequent Flyer; 60 days

Baggage

Pieces of free baggage:	3 pieces, 70 lbs.
Cost per extra bag:	$30 each
Lost baggage claims period:	45 days

Meals

Special meals available:	CH, DI, GF, HV, KO, LCA, LCH, LS, MO, SF, SR = infant, oriental, bland, low carbohydrate., fruit plate, VE, VP
Latest time to order:	24 hours advance notice

Disabled Passengers

Aisle boarding chair:	Yes
Wheelchair quota:	No, 24 hours advance notice
Seeing eye dog:	Yes
Hearing dog:	Yes
Oxygen:	Yes, carriers supply, advance notice, Service Charge
TDD service:	Yes

Pets

Charge for kennel:	$10-70
Advance notice required:	Advance notice, first come first serve

Children

Min. age to travel alone:	8, Younger needs approval
Min. age to change planes:	8, Depends
Discount available w/adult:	Yes
Discount available alone:	No
Maximum age for discount:	11
Amount of discount:	33%

PSA

Availability
States served: AZ, CA, NM, NV, OR, WA

Fares
Discount Fares: SR, MI
Advance Purchase Req.: 30, 14, 7, 2 days
Holiday blackouts: No
Frequent flyer plan: Yes
Credit cards accepted: AE, CB, DC, DI, MC, VI

Ticketing and Refunds
Bumping comp. deadline: 10 minutes
Lost ticket charge: $30.00
Min. delay on refund ticket: 4-6 Weeks

Seating
Advance seat reservation: No, fequent flyers only

Baggage
Pieces of free baggage: 3 pieces, 70 lbs.
Cost per extra bag: $15.00 each
Lost baggage claims period: 45 days

Meals
Special meals available: Snacks only
Latest time to order: N/A

Disabled Passengers
Aisle boarding chair: Yes
Wheelchair quota: No
Seeing eye dog: Yes
Hearing dog: Yes
Oxygen: No, emergency use only
TDD service: N/A

Pets

Charge for kennel:	No pets allowed
Advance notice required:	N/A

Children

Min. age to travel alone:	5
Min. age to change planes:	8
Discount available w/adult:	Yes
Discount available alone:	No
Maximum age for discount:	12
Amount of discount:	50%

PAN AMERICAN

Availability
States served: CA, CT, DC, FL, GA, HI, IL, IN, MA, MI, MN, NC, NY, OH, PA, RI, TN, TX, UT, WA

Fares
Discount Fares: SR, MI, ST, FM, RM
Advance Purchase Req.: 14, 7, 2 days
Holiday blackouts: Yes
Frequent flyer plan: Yes
Credit cards accepted: AE, CB, DC, MC, VI

Ticketing and Refunds
Bumping comp. deadline: 10 minutes
Lost ticket charge: $35.00
Min. delay on refund ticket: 6-8 weeks cash, immediate credit

Seating
Advance seat reservation: Yes, 331 days

Baggage
Pieces of free baggage: 3 pieces, 50 lbs.
Cost per extra bag: $30.00 each
Lost baggage claims period: 45 days

Meals
Special meals available: CH, DI, GF, HN, HV, HY, KO, LCA, LCH, LS, MO, SF, SR = infant, oriental, children's, VE, VP
Latest time to order: 2 hours advance notice

Disabled Passengers

Aisle boarding chair:	Yes
Wheelchair quota:	No
Seeing eye dog:	Yes
Hearing dog:	Yes
Oxygen:	Yes, carriers supply
TDD service:	No

Pets

Charge for kennel:	$25-50
Advance notice required:	24 hours

Children

Min. age to travel alone:	5
Min. age to change planes:	5
Discount available w/adult:	Yes
Discount available alone:	No
Maximum age for discount:	12, 17 in FL only
Amount of discount:	Varies

PIEDMONT

Availability

States served:	AL, CA, CO, CT, DC, FL, GA, IL, IN, KY,

LA, MA, MD, MI, MN, MO, NC, NJ,
NY, OH, PA, RI, SC, TN, TX, VA, VT,
WA, WV

Fares

Discount Fares:	FM, MI, SR, ST
Advance Purchase Req.:	30, 14, 7 days
Holiday blackouts:	Yes
Frequent flyer plan:	Yes
Credit cards accepted:	AE, CB, DC, MC, VI

Ticketing and Refunds

Bumping comp. deadline:	10 minutes
Lost ticket charge:	$30.00
Min. delay on refund ticket:	2 months

Seating

Advance seat reservation:	Yes, 29 days

Baggage

Pieces of free baggage:	3 pieces, 70 lbs.
Cost per extra bag:	$20.00 each
Lost baggage claims period:	45 days

Meals

Special meals available:	CH, DI, GF, HN, HV, HY, KO, LCA, LCH, LS, MO, SF, SR = oriental, VE, VP
Latest time to order:	24 hours advance notice

Disabled Passengers

Aisle boarding chair:	Yes
Wheelchair quota:	Yes, 4
Seeing eye dog:	Yes
Hearing dog:	Yes
Oxygen:	Yes, advance notice, service charge
TDD service:	No

Pets

Charge for kennel:	$30.00-$50.00
Advance notice required:	48 hours advance notice

Children

Min. age to travel alone:	5
Min. age to change planes:	8
Discount available w/adult:	Yes
Discount available alone:	No
Maximum age for discount:	11
Amount of discount:	Varies

TWA

Availability
States served: AL, AK, AR, AZ, CA, CO, CT,
DC, FL, GA, HI, IA, ID, IL, IN,
KS, KY, LA, MA, MD, MI, MN,
MO, NC, NE, NJ, NM, NV,
NY, OH, OK, OR, PA, RI, SD, TN, TX,
VA, WA, WI, WV

Fares
Discount Fares:	FM, MI, SR
Advance Purchase Req.:	30, 14, 7, 2 days
Holiday blackouts:	Yes
Frequent flyer plan:	Yes
Credit cards accepted:	AE, CB, DC, MC, VI

Ticketing and Refunds
Bumping comp. deadline:	10 minutes
Lost ticket charge:	$25
Min. delay on refund ticket:	20 days

Seating
Advance seat reservation:	Yes, 11 months

Baggage
Pieces of free baggage:	3 pieces, 62 lbs.
Cost per extra bag:	$20 first two
Lost baggage claims period:	45 days/4-8 weeks

Meals
Special meals available:	CH, DI, HV, KO, LCA, LCH, LS, MO, SF, SR = low carbohydrate
Latest time to order:	24 hours advance notice

Disabled Passengers

Aisle boarding chair:	Yes
Wheelchair quota:	No
Seeing eye dog:	Yes
Hearing dog:	Yes
Oxygen:	Yes, advance notice
TDD service:	No

Pets

Charge for kennel:	$30
Advance notice required:	Yes, 14 days advance notice if carried in cabin

Children

Min. age to travel alone:	5
Min. age to change planes:	8
Discount available w/adult:	Sometimes
Discount available alone:	International only
Maximum age for discount:	12
Amount of discount:	Varies

UNITED

Availability

States served:	AR, AZ, CA, CO, CT, DC, DE, FL, GA, HI, IA, ID, IL, IN, KS, KY, LA, MA, MD, ME, MI, MN, MO, MS, MT, NC, ND, NE, NH, NJ, NM, NV, NY, OH, OK, OR, PA, RI, SC, SD, TN, TX, UT, VA, VT, WA, WI, WV, WY

Fares

Discount Fares:	MI, SR, ST
Advance Purchase Req.:	7, 2 days
Holiday blackouts:	Yes
Frequent flyer plan:	Yes
Credit cards accepted:	AC, AE, CB, DC, MC, VI

Ticketing and Refunds

Bumping comp. deadline:	10 minutes
Lost ticket charge:	$35.00
Min. delay on refund ticket:	2-3 months

Seating

Advance seat reservation:	Yes, 331 days

Baggage

Pieces of free baggage:	3 pieces, 70 lbs.
Cost per extra bag:	$30.00 each
Lost baggage claims period:	45 days

Meals

Special meals available:	CH, DI, KO, LCA, LCH, LS, VP, SR = bland, infant, fruit
Latest time to order:	24 hours, 6 hours (business) advance notice

Disabled Passengers

Aisle boarding chair:	Yes
Wheelchair quota:	No
Seeing eye dog:	Yes
Hearing dog:	Yes
Oxygen:	Yes, carriers supply, extra charge, 72 hours Notice
TDD service:	Yes

Pets

Charge for kennel:	$25.00
Advance notice required:	24 hours advance notice

Children

Min. age to travel alone:	5
Min. age to change planes:	8
Discount available w/adult:	Yes
Discount available alone:	No
Maximum age for discount:	11
Amount of discount:	25% of published fares

USAir

Availability
States served: AL, AZ, CA, CO, CT, DC, DE, FL, IL, IN KY, LA, MA, MD, MI, NC, NH, NJ, NM, NV, NY, OH, PA, RI, SC, TN, TX, VA, VT, WI, WV

Fares
Discount Fares:	FA, MI, SR
Advance Purchase Req.:	30, 14, 7 days
Holiday blackouts:	Yes
Frequent flyer plan:	Yes
Credit cards accepted:	AE, CB, DC, MC, VI

Ticketing and Refunds
Bumping comp. deadline:	10 minutes
Lost ticket charge:	$30.00
Min. delay on refund ticket:	1 month

Seating
Advance seat reservation:	Yes, 21 days

Baggage
Pieces of free baggage:	3 pieces, 70 lbs.
Cost per extra bag:	$20.00 each
Lost baggage claims period:	45 days

Meals
Special meals available:	CH, DI, GF, HY, KO, LCA, LCH, LS, VE, VP
Latest time to order:	N/A

Disabled Passengers	
Aisle boarding chair:	Yes
Wheelchair quota:	No
Seeing eye dog:	Yes
Hearing dog:	Yes
Oxygen:	Yes, advance notice
TDD service:	Yes

Pets	
Charge for kennel:	$10.00-$50.00
Advance notice required:	24 hours advance notice

Children	
Min. age to travel alone:	5
Min. age to change planes:	8
Discount available w/adult:	Yes
Discount available alone:	No
Maximum age for discount:	12
Amount of discount:	25%

17

AIRPORT PROFILES

O ne of the most important factors in determining how smooth your flight will be is the airport you take off from, land at, or fly through. This section contains detailed information on what you can expect to find at most major airports.

The airports are listed alphabetically by city, and each table includes the official name of the airport and its airport code. These codes can help you in deciphering reservations and tracking down baggage that may have been lost at a particular airport.

The tables also include specific information on the facilities available at each of the airports, as well as car rental and car parking information.

An important factor in determining what you can expect at an airport is how busy it is. The more passengers the airport handles, the more hectic you can expect your experience there to be. The tables list the number of passengers that typically pass through the airport each year. In order to help you get your bearing when you arrive, we have listed the approximate distance from downtown and the cost and frequency of various types of transportation downtown.

All too often, because of weather conditions and other factors, your flight may be diverted to another airport. We have listed the diversion airports where you may end up if your destination airport is closed.

ATLANTA

William B. Hartsfield Atlanta International Airport

Airport Code:	ATL
Location from City:	10 miles south
Annual Traffic:	45,000,000 passengers (1986)
Diversion Airports:	1. Charleston 2. Charlotte 3. Greenville 4. Birmingham 5. Jacksonville
Facilities:	Bar 9 a.m. to 2 a.m.; Buffet 24 hours; Restaurant 11 a.m. to 12 a.m.; Bank 9 a.m. to 10 p.m.; Drop boxes and postage vending machines.
Car Rental:	Alamo, Avis, Budget, Dollar, General, Hertz, National
Car Parking	Short term: $1/hour $6.00/day max.; Long term: $3/day
Airline Clubs:	Crown, Ionosphere, many others
Trans. to Downtown:	By coach every 15 min. all day, $7.00 one way/$12.00 RT; By bus every 30 minutes from 5 a.m. to 11 p.m., $.75; By taxi $13.50
Check-in Time:	Domestic 45 min.; International 90 min.

BALTIMORE

Baltimore-Washington International Airport

Airport Code:	BWI
Location from City:	10 miles southwest
Annual Traffic:	8,670,506 passengers (1986)
Diversion Airports:	1. Philadelphia 2. Washington-Dulles
Facilities:	24-hour snack bar pier D; Restaurant 11 a.m. to 10 p.m.; Lounges 9 a.m. to 2 a.m.; Self-service Post Office 24 hours
Car Rental:	Avis, Budget, Dollar, Hertz, National
Car Parking	Short term: $1.00/30 minutes; Long--term: first hour $3.00, 1 to 24 hours $6.00; Each add. day 0 to 6 hrs. $3.00, 6 to 24 hrs. $6.00
Airline Clubs:	Crown, Ionosphere, Omaha of Nebraska Business Service Center, Red Carpet
Trans. to Downtown:	**Baltimore** – By coach, $5.00/30 min.; By taxi $12.00; Amtrak $5.75; MARC Commuter Rail $2.70, during morning and evening rush hours **Washington** – By coach $12.00 every hour; By taxi $33.00; Amtrak $9.00; MARC Commuter Rail $4.30 during morning and evening rush hours.
Check-in Time:	30 min.

BOSTON	
Logan International	
Airport Code:	BOS
Location from City:	5 miles north
Annual Traffic:	21,900,000 passengers (1986)
Diversion Airports:	1. Hartford 2. Bangor
Facilities:	Bar 11 a.m. to 2 a.m.; Buffet 7 a.m. to 11 p.m.; Restaurant 12 p.m. to 8 p.m.; Bank Drive-in
Car Rental:	Alamo, Ajax, Avis, Budget, Dollar, Hertz, National
Car Parking	Short term: $2.00/hour, $10.00/day max.
Airline Clubs:	Admirals, Ambassador, Circle, Crown, Executive, Maharajah, Red Carpet, Senator, Tara
Trans. to Downtown:	By coach $5.25, every hour, from 9 a.m. to 11 p.m.; By train $0.60, every 10 minutes from 5:30 a.m. to 1:30 a.m.; By taxi $12.00
Check-in Time:	Domestic 45 min.; International 1.5 hrs.

CHICAGO
O'Hare International

Airport Code:	ORD
Location from City:	23 miles northwest
Annual Traffic:	54,770,673 passengers (1986)
Diversion Airports:	1. Grand Rapids 2. Indianapolis
Facilities:	Bar 10 a.m. to 11 p.m.; Snack Bar and Restaurant 24 hours; Bank, Foreign Currency Exchange 10 a.m. to 8 p.m.
Car Rental:	Avis, Budget, Hertz, National
Car Parking	Short term: $1.00/hour, $9.00/day max.; Long term: $4.00/day
Airline Clubs:	Admirals, Ambassador, Clipper, Crown, Executive, Ionosphere, Red Carpet, Rembrandt, Scanorama, Senator, Speedwing, Top Flight
Trans. to Downtown:	By coach 24 hours every 15 minutes, rate varies; By taxi $18.20; By Rail, CT, $1.00 every 10 minutes; By bus $9.00 to $10.00
Check-in Time:	45 min.

CLEVELAND
Hopkins International

Airport Code:	CLE
Location from City:	12 miles southwest
Annual Traffic:	6,581,614 passengers (1986)
Diversion Airports:	Airline Preference
Facilities:	Restaurant/Cocktail Lounge 11 a.m. to 9 p.m.; Cafeteria 24 hours; Society National Bank M-Th 10 a.m. to 2:30 p.m., F 10 a.m. to 4 p.m.; Post Office 24 hours
Car Rental:	Avis, Budget, Dollar, Hertz, National
Car Parking	Short term: $1.00/hour, $9.00/day max.; Long Term: $5.00/day
Airline Clubs:	Admirals, Red Carpet, Top Flight
Trans. to Downtown:	Hopkins limousine $15.00, reservations only 24 hours; Rapid Transit $1.00, 24 hours every 15 minutes; taxi $15.00 to $17.00
Check-in Time:	45 min.

DALLAS
Dallas/Fort Worth Regional

Airport Code:	DFW
Location from City:	17 miles
Annual Traffic:	34,945,326 passengers (1986)
Diversion Airports:	1. San Antonio 2. Houston
Facilities:	Bar 7 a.m. to 11 p.m.; Buffet 6 a.m. to 10 p.m.; Restaurant 5:30 a.m. to 9 p.m.; Post Office 7 a.m. to 8 p.m.
Car Rental:	Avis, Budget, Hertz, National
Car Parking	Short term: $.75/hour,$7.00/day max.; Long term: $4.00/day
Airline Clubs:	Admirals, Crown
Trans. to Downtown:	**Dallas** – By coach $10.00 every 30 minutes from 6 a.m. to 10 p.m.; By taxi $22.50; **Fort Worth** – By coach $6.00 every 35 minutes from 6:01 a.m. to 10:50 p.m.; By taxi $22.50
Check-in Time:	45 min.

DENVER
Stapleton International

Airport Code:	DEN
Location from City:	8 miles northeast
Annual Traffic:	34,500,006 passengers (1986)
Diversion Airports:	1. Colorado Springs 2. Salt Lake City
Facilities:	Bar 6 a.m. to 2 a.m.; Buffet 24 hours; Restaurant 11 a.m. to 9 p.m.; Bank and Post Office 8 a.m. to 5 p.m.
Car Rental:	Avis, Budget, Dollar, Hertz, National
Car Parking	Short term: $1.00/hour, $7.00/day max.; Long term: $3.00/day
Airline Clubs:	Ambassador, Council, Crown, Horizon, Red Carpet
Trans. to Downtown:	By coach $2.30 every 15 minutes from 7 a.m. to 9 p.m.; By bus $.50 every 20 minutes from 6 a.m. to 8 p.m.; By taxi $9.00
Check-in Time:	45 min.

DETROIT
Detroit Metropolitan

Airport Code:	DTW
Location from City:	17 miles west
Annual Traffic:	8,923,297 enplaning passengers (1986); 8,681,286 deplaning passengers (1986)
Diversion Airports:	1. Windsor 2. Grand Rapids
Facilities:	Bar; Buffet; Restaurant
Car Rental:	Avis, Budget, Dollar, Hertz, National
Car Parking	Short term: $12.00/day; Long term: $2.50/day
Airline Clubs:	Admirals, Clipper, Crown, Executive, Red Carpet, World
Trans. to Downtown:	By limousine $9.00 every 30 minutes; By taxi $28.00
Check-in Time:	45 min.

HONOLULU
International (John Rodgers Terminal)

Airport Code:	HNL
Location from City:	9 miles northwest
Annual Traffic:	18,000,000 passengers (1986)
Diversion Airports:	1. Hilo 2. Maui
Facilities:	Bar 8 a.m. to 2 a.m.; Fresh Express Caf 24 hours; Restaurant 11:30 a.m. to 2:30 p.m. and 6 p.m. to 10 p.m.; Bank 8:30 a.m. to 3 p.m.; Post Office 8 a.m. to 8:30 p.m. (next to airport)
Car Rental:	Avis, Budget, Dollar, Hertz
Car Parking	Short term: $.50 first 30 minutes, $.75 each add. hour; Long term: $6.00/day
Airline Clubs:	Admirals, Captains, Crown, Empress, Mabuhay, Morning Calm, Red Carpet, Sakura, Silver Kris, World
Trans. to Downtown:	By coach $5.00 meets all arrivals; By bus $.60 every 30 minutes; By taxi $15.00
Check-in Time:	Domestic 60 min.; International 1.5 hrs.

HOUSTON
Intercontinental

Airport Code:	IAH
Location from City:	22 miles south
Annual Traffic:	14,400,000 passengers (1986)
Diversion Airports:	1. Hobby-Houston 2. New Orleans 3. San Antonio
Facilities:	Banking Machine available; Bar Terminals A and B 11 a.m. to 8 p.m.; Terminal C 11 a.m. to 9 p.m.; Buffeteria Terminals A, B, C-South 24 hours, C North 6:30 a.m. to 9 p.m.; Post Office 24 hours
Car Rental:	Avis, Budget, Dollar, Hertz, National
Car Parking	Short term: $2.00 first 90 minutes; Long term: $4.00/day max.
Airline Clubs:	Crown, Ionosphere
Trans. to Downtown:	By taxi $22.50; By bus $7.50 one-way every 30 minutes from 5:30 a.m. to 12:30 a.m.
Check-in Time:	45 min.

INDIANAPOLIS
International

Airport Code:	IND
Location from City:	7 miles southwest
Annual Traffic:	4,200,000 passengers (1986)
Diversion Airports:	1. O'Hare-Chicago 2. St. Louis
Facilities:	Bar 11 a.m. to 2 a.m.; Buffet 24 hours; Restaurant 11 a.m. to 9 p.m.; Bank 9 a.m. to 5 p.m.
Car Rental:	Avis, Budget, Dollar, Hertz, National
Car Parking	Short term: $9.00/day; Long term: $2.50/day
Trans. to Downtown:	By bus $1.05 every 30 minutes from 5 a.m. to 11:45 p.m.; By taxi $10.50
Check-in Time:	30 min.

KANSAS CITY, MISSOURI
International

Airport Code:	MCI
Location from City:	18 miles northwest
Annual Traffic:	8,299.388 passengers (1986)
Diversion Airports:	1. Omaha 2. St. Louis
Facilities:	Bar 9 a.m. to 9 p.m. (varies); Restaurant 7 a.m. to 9 p.m. (varies); Snack Bars 24 hours; Bank 9 a.m. to 5 p.m.
Car Rental:	Avis, Budget, Dollar, Hertz, National
Car Parking	Short term: $.50/hour; Long term: $5.00 to $12.00/day
Airline Clubs:	Admirals, Ambassador, Ionosphere
Trans. to Downtown:	By coach $9.00 every 30 minutes between 5:45 a.m. and 11:30 p.m. from Gate 63, Terminal C; By taxi $26.00
Check-in Time:	45 min.

LAS VEGAS
McCarran International

Airport Code:	LAS
Location from City:	5 miles south
Annual Traffic:	12,303,400 passengers (1986); 14,000,000 est. (1987)
Diversion Airports:	1. Los Angeles 2. Phoenix
Facilities:	Bar and Buffet 24 hours; Restaurant 6:30 a.m. to 8 p.m.; Bank 10 a.m. to 3 p.m.; Post Office 8:30 a.m. to 8 p.m.
Car Rental:	Allstate, Avis, Dollar, Hertz, National, SavMor
Car Parking	$1.00/hour, $6/day max. covered, $4.00/day max. open air; Monthly $72 covered, $48 open-air
Trans. to Downtown:	By coach $4.25 every 10 minutes from 6 a.m. to 12 a.m.; By taxi $15.00
Check-in Time:	Domestic 30 min.; International 1 hr.

LOS ANGELES
International

Airport Code:	LAX
Location from City:	15 miles southwest
Annual Traffic:	41,417,867 passengers (1986)
Diversion Airports:	1. Las Vegas 2. Ontario
Facilities:	Bar and Coffee Shops 6 a.m. to 2 a.m.; Restaurant M-F 11 a.m. to 2:30 p.m. and 6 p.m. to 10 p.m., Sat 10 a.m. to 3 p.m. and 6 p.m. to 11 p.m., Sun 4:30 p.m. to 10:30 p.m.; Bank M-F 9 a.m. to 3 p.m.; Snack bar 7 a.m. to 11 p.m.
Car Rental:	Avis, Budget, Dollar, Hertz, National
Car Parking	Short term: $1.00/hour, $10/day max.; Long term: $4.00/day
Airline Clubs:	Admirals, Ambassador, Clipper, Horizon, Maple Leaf, Red Carpet, Royal Viking, Sakura, Sun King, Varig
Trans. to Downtown:	By RTD Airport Express Coach $4.50; By RTD Airport Express Coach to San Bernardino Greyhound bus station $8.00; All RTD lines board in front of terminals 2-7. Tickets may be purchased at the information booths in front of the baggage claim area, or exact fare may be paid to the driver.; 24-hour information line 213-626-4455 or 213-973-1222; By RTD bus $.45 to $1.35 board mini-bus outside of terminals 2-7 every 10 minutes from 5 a.m. to 1 a.m. for trip to transfer depot for direct connections to the Greater Los Angeles area; By taxi $9.00 to $18.00.
Check-in Time:	45 min.

MEMPHIS
International

Airport Code:	MEM
Location from City:	10 miles southeast
Annual Traffic:	8,677,014 passengers (1986)
Diversion Airports:	Airline preference
Facilities:	Bar 8 a.m. to 10 p.m.; Buffet 24 hours; Restaurant 11 a.m. to 9 p.m.; Union Planters automatic teller
Car Rental:	Avis, Budget, Hertz, National on premises; Also available: Alamo, Dollar, Kirk, Payless, Snoopy, Thrifty
Car Parking	Short term: $12.00/day; Long term: $6.00/day; Reduced Rate: $4.00/day
Airline Clubs:	Crown, Top Flight
Trans. to Downtown:	By coach $5.00 on demand; By taxi $13.00
Check-in Time:	1 hr.

MIAMI	
International	
Airport Code:	MIA
Location from City:	8 miles west
Annual Traffic:	22 million passengers (1986)
Diversion Airports:	1. West Palm Beach 2. Fort Lauderdale
Facilities:	Bar 10 a.m. to 8 p.m.; Buffet 24 hours; Airport Hotel 305-871-4100; Bank M-F 9 a.m. to 4 p.m., Sat. 9 a.m. to 12 p.m.; Post Office M-F 8:30 a.m. to 5 p.m., Sat. 8:30 a.m. to 12 p.m.
Car Rental:	Avis, Dollar, Hertz, National
Car Parking	Short term: $1.00/30 minutes, $15.00/day max.; Long term: $1.00/hour, $5.00/day max.
Airline Clubs:	Clipper, Club America, Crown, Ionosphere
Trans. to Downtown:	By coach $6.75 every 10 minutes, 24 hours; By bus $.75 every 30 minutes from 5:27 a.m. to 8:26 p.m.; By taxi $12.00
Check-in Time:	45 min.

MILWAUKEE
General Mitchell International Airport

Airport Code:	MKE
Location from City:	6 miles south
Annual Traffic:	3,500,000 passengers (1986)
Diversion Airports:	1. Chicago 2. Minneapolis
Facilities:	Bar 10 a.m. to 11 p.m.; Coffee Shop 24 hours; Restaurant 11:30 a.m. to 8 p.m.
Car Rental:	Alamo, Avis, Budget, Dollar, Hertz, National
Car Parking	Short term: $.75/30 minutes, $6.50/day max.; Long term: $2.00/day
Airline Clubs:	Top Flight
Trans. to Downtown:	By coach $6.00 every 30 minutes from 7 a.m. to 11:15 p.m.; By bus $1.00 every 30 minutes from 6:00 a.m. to 6 p.m.; By taxi $14.00
Check-in Time:	30 min.

MINNEAPOLIS
Minneapolis-Saint Paul International

Airport Code:	MSP
Location from City:	7.5 miles southeast of Minneapolis; 7 miles southwest of St.Paul
Annual Traffic:	17,073,605 passengers (1986)
Diversion Airports:	1. Duluth 2. Milwaukee
Facilities:	Bar open 8 a.m. to 1 a.m.; Restaurant 5:30 a.m. to 10 p.m.; Post Office 24 hours
Car Rental:	Avis, Budget, Dollar, Hertz, National
Car Parking	Short term: $1.00/hour; Long term: $10.00/day
Airline Clubs:	Horizon, Top Flight
Trans. to Downtown:	By limosine $6.50 every 15 minutes from 5 a.m. to 11 p.m.; By taxi $17.00
Check-in Time:	30 min.

NASHVILLE
Metropolitan

Airport Code:	BNA
Location from City:	10 miles southeast
Annual Traffic:	4,544,444 passengers (1986)
Diversion Airports:	1.Memphis 2.Atlanta
Facilities:	Bar 11 a.m. to 10 p.m.; Buffet 6 a.m. to 11 p.m.; Restaurant 11:30 a.m. to 9 p.m.; Bank 9 a.m. to 4 p.m.; Post Office 24 hours
Car Rental:	Alamo, Avis, Budget, Dollar, Hertz, National
Car Parking	Short term: $1.00 first hour., each add. hour $2.00; $8.00/day max.; Long term: $4.50/day
Trans. to Downtown:	By coach $8.50 on call; By bus $.75, $.10 for transfers, every hour from 6 a.m. to 12 a.m.; By taxi $11.00
Check-in Time:	45 min.

NEW ORLEANS
International (Moisant Field)

Airport Code:	MSY
Location from City:	13 miles west
Annual Traffic:	5,401,000 passengers (1986)
Diversion Airports:	1. Memphis 2. Houston
Facilities:	Bar 8 a.m. to 10 p.m.; Buffet 24 hours; Restaurant 11 a.m. to 9 p.m.; Post Office 9 a.m. to 5 p.m.
Car Rental:	Avis, Budget, Dollar, Hertz, National
Car Parking	Short term: $2.00/first hour, $1.00 each add. hour; Long term: $5.00/day
Airline Clubs:	Crown, Ionosphere
Trans. to Downtown:	By coach $7.00 every 15 minutes; By bus $.90 from 6:30 a.m. to 12 a.m.; By taxi $18.00
Check-in Time:	Domestic 45 min.; International 1.5 hrs.

NEW YORK CITY
La Guardia

Airport Code:	LGA
Location from City:	8 miles east
Annual Traffic:	22,000,000 passengers (1986)
Diversion Airports:	1. Newark-New Jersey 2. National--Washington 3. JFK-New York
Facilities:	Bar 11 a.m. to 12 a.m.; Buffet 7 a.m. to 11 p.m.; Restaurant 24 hours; Bank 9 a.m. to 5 p.m.; Post Office 8 a.m. to 5 p.m.
Car Rental:	Avis, Budget, Dollar, Hertz, National
Car Parking	$3.00 first two hours, each add. hour $1.00; $15.00/day max.
Airline Clubs:	Admirals, Ambassador, Crown Room, Ionosphere, Red Carpet
Trans. to Downtown:	By coach $5.00 every 30 minutes from 6:45 a.m. to 12:01 a.m.; By bus and subway $2.00, take Q48 bus to Main St. subway station, Flushing (Long Island R.R.; station) at corner of Main St. and Roosevelt Ave., then subway IRT 7 to; Times Square, Manhattan
Check-in Time:	30 min.

NEW YORK CITY/NEW JERSEY
Newark International

Airport Code:	EWR
Location from City:	16 miles southwest
Annual Traffic:	29,000,000 passengers (1986)
Diversion Airports:	1. Baltimore 2. Montreal
Facilities:	Bar 9:30 a.m. to 1 a.m.; Buffet 6:30 a.m. to 9 p.m.; Bank 9 a.m. to 5 p.m.
Car Rental:	Avis, Budget, Dollar, Hertz, National
Car Parking	Short term: $2.00/hour; Long term: $5.00/day
Airline Clubs:	Ambassador, Crown, Ionosphere, Red Carpet, Sun King
Trans. to Downtown:	By coach $5.00 every 30 minutes from 7 a.m. to 12 a.m.; By Airport Express bus $5.00 every 30 minutes from 6:30 a.m. to 12 a.m.; By train $3.00 every 20-30 minutes from 6:20 a.m. to 11:15 p.m. M-F, 6:40 a.m. to 12:10 a.m. weekends (Airlink mini-coach at terminals A and B to Penn Station Newark) then $1.00 Conrail train every 20 minutes from 6:20 a.m. to 9 p.m. to Penn Central Station, 34th and 8th Ave.; By taxi $23.50-$28.00 flat rate plus all tolls
Check-in Time:	45 min.

NEW YORK CITY
John F. Kennedy International

Airport Code:	JFK
Location from City:	15 miles southeast
Annual Traffic:	24,900,000 passengers (1986)
Diversion Airports:	1. Newark-New York 2. La Guardia-New York
Facilities:	Bars 8 a.m. to 11:30 p.m.; Snack stands 6 a.m. to 10:30 p.m.; Coffee shops 6 a.m. to 11:30 p.m.; Restaurants 6:30 a.m. to 10 p.m.; Cafeteria 24 hours; Banks hours vary by terminal; Postal vending machines
Car Rental:	Avis, Budget, Dollar, Hertz, National
Car Parking	Short term: $3.00 first two hours; each add. hour $1.00; Long term: $5.00/day
Airline Clubs:	Admirals, Ambassador, Clipper, Executive (Monarch), Ionosphere, Maharaja, Red Carpet, Royal Viking, Sabena, Sun King
Trans. to Downtown:	By coach $5.00 to $11.00 every 20-30 minutes from 5:20 a.m. to 1 a.m.; By bus and subway $1.00 every 10 minutes from 6:30 a.m. to 7 p.m., every 30 minutes, from 7 p.m. to 6:30 a.m.; By JFK Express $6.50 every 20 minutes from 5:30 a.m. to 12:30 a.m.; By taxi $28.00 plus tolls
Check-in Time:	45 min., varies during high traffic times

ORLANDO
International (McCoy Field)

Airport Code:	MCO
Location from City:	8 miles southeast
Annual Traffic:	12,495,346 passengers (1986)
Diversion Airports:	1. Tampa International 2. Daytona Beach Regional
Facilities:	Bar 10 a.m. to 12 a.m., varies with location; Buffet 24 hours, varies with location; Restaurant 24 hours; Bank 8 a.m. to 5 p.m.
Car Rental:	Avis, Budget, Dollar, Hertz, National, Superior
Car Parking	Short term: $1.00/45 minutes; Long term: $2/8 hours, $5.00/day max.
Airline Clubs:	Clipper, Crown, Ionosphere
Trans. to Downtown:	By coach $5.00 24 hours every 15 minutes; By bus $.65 every 60 minutes from 6:30 a.m. to 7:30 p.m.; By taxi $24.00
Check-in Time:	20-60 min., 1.5 hrs. on holidays

PHOENIX
Sky Harbor International

Airport Code:	PHX
Location from City:	4 miles east
Annual Traffic:	5,931,000 passengers (1986)
Diversion Airports:	1. Tucson 2. Albuquerque
Facilities:	Bar; Buffet; Restaurant; Bank
Car Rental:	Avis, Budget, Dollar, Hertz, National
Car Parking	Short term: $10.00/day; Long term: $3.00/day
Trans. to Downtown:	By taxi $5.00 to $10.00
Check-in Time:	30 min.

PHILADELPHIA
International

Airport Code:	PHL
Location from City:	8 miles southwest
Annual Traffic:	14,000,000 passengers (1986)
Diversion Airports:	1. JFK-New York 2. Baltimore/Washington 3. Newark Airport
Facilities:	Bars 8:00 a.m. to 12 a.m.; Buffet 6 a.m. to 10:30 p.m.; Snack Bar 24 hours; Restaurant 11:30 a.m. to 8:30 p.m.; Post Office 24 hours automated
Car Rental:	Avis, Budget, Dollar, Hertz. National
Car Parking	Short term: $12.00/day; Long term: $6.00/day
Airline Clubs:	Ambassador, Crown Room, Ionosphere, Red Carpet, USAir
Trans. to Downtown:	By coach $4.00 every 30 minutes from 6 a.m. to 12 a.m.; By limousine $6.00 to hotels, $12.00 door-to-door; By taxi $15.00
Check-in Time:	45-60 min.

PITTSBURGH

Greater Pittsburgh International

Airport Code:	PIT
Location from City:	16 miles northwest
Annual Traffic:	15,989,507 passengers (1986)
Facilities:	Bar 9 a.m. to 1 a.m.; Buffet 24 hours; Restaurant 11 a.m. to 8 p.m.; Bank 9:30 a.m. to 4 p.m.; Post Office 8 a.m. to 5 p.m.
Car Rental:	Avis, Budget, Hertz, National
Car Parking	Short term: $1.75/hour; Long term: $5.25/day
Airline Clubs:	Ambassador, British Air, Crown, Ionosphere, Red Carpet, USAir
Trans. to Downtown:	By coach $3.25 every 30 minutes from 5 a.m. to 11 p.m.; By taxi $16.00
Check-in Time:	30 min.

PORTLAND

International

Airport Code:	PDX
Location from City:	9 miles northeast
Annual Traffic:	5,107,900 passengers (1986)
Diversion Airports:	1. Seattle 2. Spokane
Facilities:	Bar 10 a.m. to 1:30 a.m.; Restaurant 5:45 a.m. to 11 p.m.; Coffee Shop 5.45 a.m. to 2 p.m.; Dining Room 5 p.m. to 11 p.m.
Car Rental:	Avis, Budget, Dollar, Hertz, National
Car Parking	Short term: $.50 per/30 minutes; Long term: $5.00/day; Economy $18.00/week, $3.00/day
Airline Clubs:	Crown, Red Carpet
Trans. to Downtown:	RAZ $5.00 every 20 minutes from 5:30 a.m. to 12 a.m.; By bus $.85; By taxi $20.00 to $23.00
Check-in Time:	1 hr.

ST. LOUIS

Lambert International

Airport Code:	STL
Location from City:	15 miles northwest
Annual Traffic:	10,184,625 passengers (1986)
Diversion Airports:	1. Indianapolis 2. Kansas City
Facilities:	Bar 6:30 a.m. to 1 a.m.; Buffet 5:30 a.m. to 11:30 p.m.; Restaurant 11:00 a.m. to 8:45 p.m.; Post Office 8:30 a.m. to 10:30 a.m.
Car Rental:	Avis, Budget, Dollar, Hertz, National
Car Parking	Short term: $.50/hour; Long term: $3.00/day
Airline Clubs:	Admirals, Ambassador, Ionosphere
Trans. to Downtown:	By coach $6.00 every 30 minutes; By taxi $17.00
Check-in Time:	45 min.

SALT LAKE CITY

International

Airport Code:	SLC
Location from City:	7 miles west
Annual Traffic:	9,991,000 passengers (1986)
Diversion Airports:	1. Denver 2. Las Vegas
Facilities:	Bar 11 a.m. to 9 p.m.; Buffet 24 hours; Restaurant 6:30 a.m. to 9 p.m.; Bank 9 a.m. to 6 p.m.
Car Rental:	Avis, Budget, Dollar, Hertz, National
Car Parking	Short term: $.75/hour, $4.85 per day; Long term: $2.85/day
Airline Clubs:	Crown
Trans. to Downtown:	By coach $1.75; By bus $.50 every 30 minutes; By taxi $7.50
Check-in Time:	20 min.

SAN DIEGO

International (Lindbergh Field)

Airport Code:	SAN
Location from City:	3 miles northwest
Annual Traffic:	10,500,000 passengers (1986)
Diversion Airports:	1. Los Angeles 2. Ontario 3. John Wayne
Facilities:	Bar 6:00 a.m. to 12 a.m.; Buffet 24 hours; Restaurant 6 a.m. to 11 p.m.; Bank 8:30 a.m. to 5:30 p.m.
Car Rental:	Avis, Budget, General, Hertz, National
Car Parking	Short term: $1.00/hour, $8.00/day max.; after two days $10.00/day max.; Long term: $5.00/day
Trans. to Downtown:	By coach $1.50 from 6 a.m. to 12 a.m.; By bus $1.00 every 20 minutes from 6 a.m. to 1 a.m.; By taxi $5.00
Check-in Time:	30 min.

SAN FRANCISCO

International

Airport Code:	SFO
Location from City:	16 miles southeast
Annual Traffic:	28,607,363 passengers (1986)
Diversion Airports:	1. Los Angeles 2. Oakland 3. San Jose
Facilities:	Bar 7 a.m. to 1 a.m.; Buffet 6 a.m. to 11:30 p.m.; Restaurant 10 a.m. to 10 p.m.; Bank 8:30 a.m. to 5 p.m. M-F; Post Office 24 hours
Car Rental:	Avis, Budget, Dollar, Hertz, National
Car Parking	Short term: $1.00/hour; Long term: $7.00/day
Airline Clubs:	Admirals, Ambassador, Captains, Clipper, Crown, Dynasty, Empress, Golden Aztec, Horizon, Ionosphere, Mabuhay, Red Carpet, Sakura, Senator, Silver Kris, Top Flight
Trans. to Downtown:	By coach $6.00 every 15 minutes from 6 a.m. to 10 p.m., every 30 minutes from 10 p.m. to 6 a.m.; By bus $1.25 every 30 minutes from 5:45 a.m. to 1:30 a.m.; By taxi $24.00; By van $7.00
Check-in Time:	1 hr.

SEATTLE

Seattle Tacoma International

Airport Code:	SEA
Location from City:	13 miles south
Annual Traffic:	13,600,000 passengers (1986)
Diversion Airports:	1. King County International (Boeing Field) 2. Portland
Facilities:	Bar 6 a.m. to 2 a.m.; Buffet 6 a.m. to 1 a.m.; Restaurant 6 a.m. to 11 p.m.
Car Rental:	Avis, Budget, Dollar, Hertz, Mini, National, Rate
Car Parking	First 30 minutes free, $2.00/hour, $7.00/day max.
Airline Clubs:	Admirals, Board Room, Horizon, Red Carpet, Royal Pacific, Scanorama Lounge, Thai Royal, Top Flight
Trans. to Downtown:	By coach $5.00 every 30 minutes from 6 a.m. to 12 a.m.; By bus $1.00 every 15 minutes from 5:30 a.m. to 1:20 a.m.; By taxi $23.00
Check-in Time:	1 hr.

TAMPA	
International	
Airport Code:	TPA
Location from City:	5 miles west
Annual Traffic:	10,000,000 passengers (1986)
Diversion Airports:	1. Orlando 2. St. Petersburg/Clearwater
Facilities:	Bar; Buffet 6:30 a.m. to 12 a.m.; Restaurant; Hotel
Car Rental:	Avis, Budget, Dollar, Hertz, National
Car Parking	$.50/hr., $5.00/day
Trans. to Downtown:	By taxi $8.00
Check-in Time:	60 min.

WASHINGTON DC

Dulles International

Airport Code:	IAD
Location from City:	27 miles west
Annual Traffic:	10,943,565 passengers (1986)
Diversion Airports:	1. Baltimore 2. Philadelphia
Facilities:	Cocktail Bar 10 a.m. to 12 a.m.; Restaurant/Snack bar 24 hours; Bank M-F 9 a.m. to 1 p.m. and 3 p.m. to 5 p.m.; Post Office M-F 9 a.m. to 5 p.m., Sat. 9 a.m. to 12 p.m.
Car Rental:	Avis, Budget, Dollar, Hertz, National
Car Parking	Short-term: $1.50/hour, $26/day max.; Long-term: $1.00/hour, $6.00/day max.; Satellite $4.00/day; Valet $25.00/first day, each add. day $10.00
Airline Clubs:	Admirals, Ambassador, Clipper, Concorde, Red Carpet
Trans. to Downtown:	By coach $11.00 every 30 minutes from 5 a.m. to 1 a.m.; By taxi $31.00
Check-in Time:	45 min.

WASHINGTON DC

National

Airport Code:	DCA
Location from City:	3 miles southwest
Annual Traffic:	15,200,000 passengers (1986)
Facilities:	Bar 7 a.m. to 10 p.m.; Snack Bar 24 hours; Restaurant 7 a.m. to 9 p.m.
Car Rental:	Avis, Budget, Dollar, Hertz
Car Parking	General: $1.50/hour, $7.50/day max.; Short term: $2.00/hour, $20.00/day max.; Long term: $.75/hour, $6.00/day max.
Airline Clubs:	Ambassador, Red Carpet
Trans. to Downtown:	By taxi $6.70 to $7.70; By Washington Flyer bus $5.00 to $8.00 every 30 minutes; By metrorail $.80 to $1.05 every 5-10 minutes; By limousine, airport connection $6.00/person introductory rate
Check-in Time:	30-45 min.

AUTHORS

Stephen Brobeck is the Executive Director of the Consumer Federation of America. He earned a Ph.D. in American Studies from the University of Pennsylvania and is listed in *Who's Who in America*. He serves on the Board of Directors for the Institute for Civil Justice, National Center for Financial Services, Joint Council on Economic Education, Citizens for Tax Justice, National Committee for Responsive Philanthropy, National Coalition for Consumer Education, Public Voice for Food and Health Policy, and is on the Advisory Committee of the Electric Power Research Institute. Brobeck is co-author of *The Bank Book* and *The Product Safety Book*, and is a regular contributor to newspaper editorial pages. He has written a series of consumer pamphlets including *Your Credit Options, Your Savings Options*, and *Saving through Store Brands*.

Jack Gillis is Director of Public Affairs for the Consumer Federation of America and is a member of the faculty of The George Washington University, where he teaches Marketing and Public Policy. He is author of *The Car Book, The Used Car Book*, and *How to Make Your Car Last (Almost) Forever*, co-author of *The Childwise Catalog: A Consumer Guide to Buying the Safest and Best Products for Your Children* and *The Armchair Mechanic*, editor of *The Bank Book* and *The Product Safety Book*, and writes two monthly columns for *Good Housekeeping*.

The *Consumer Federation of America* is composed of more than 230 organizations representing over 50 million Americans. As a consumer advocacy organization, CFA is committed to the goals of consumer advocacy and education. CFA member groups include grassroots, consumer, senior citizen, rural, labor, cooperative and other organizations. Established in 1968 CFA advances pro-consumer policy before Congress, the Administration and regulatory agencies. It assists state and local groups and increases public and media awareness of consumer needs.